PRAISE FOR

.|

"Massimo Faggioli's brilliant contributions to the reception of Vatican II are rooted in careful historical research and the posing of insightful questions. His prose not only continues to capture the vitality of the council, but effectively shows how the council persists beyond its texts as a programmatic 'event' that continues to shape the future."

—Mary Ann Hinsdale, IHM
Boston College

"Learned, with a deep sense for the European church and some pointed observations for the U.S., Massimo Faggioli is the voice of a fresh approach to ecclesiology. Of particular value is Faggioli's generous embrace of the whole of the church, from the Sunday folks in the pew, to the multiple expressions of the lay movements, to the full sweep of the hierarchy—all addressed with a complex understanding of history and culture."

—Nancy Dallavalle
Fairfield University

"Few scholars can match Massimo Faggioli's mastery of the history of the Second Vatican Council and its background. While at times some find his perspective contentious, readers can trust that it arises out of comprehensive, firsthand knowledge of the sources, primary and secondary, in all the languages pertinent to the council. Faggioli's writings on the contemporary Catholic Church are not to be missed."

—David G. Schultenover, SJ
Marquette University

"Massimo Faggioli is an outstanding scholar who is widely regarded throughout the Catholic world as among the most important interpreters of the Second Vatican Council. Grounded in meticulous scholarship, his historical judgments are always balanced and insightful."

—Ormond Rush
Australian Catholic University

THE
RISING
LAITY

Ecclesial
Movements
since
Vatican II

MASSIMO FAGGIOLI

Paulist Press
New York / Mahwah, NJ

Permission for the use of previously published material may be found in the acknowledgments.

Cover image by Natykach Nataliia / Shutterstock.com
Cover and book design by Lynn Else

Library of Congress Cataloging-in-Publication Data

Faggioli, Massimo.
    The rising laity : ecclesial movements since Vatican II / Massimo Faggioli.
      pages cm
    Includes bibliographical references and index.
      ISBN 978-0-8091-4934-6 (pbk. : alk. paper) — ISBN 978-1-58768-523-1 (ebook)
      1. Vatican Council (2nd : 1962-1965 : Basilica di San Pietro in Vaticano) 2. Church renewal—Catholic Church. I. Title.
      BX8301962 .F26 2016
      262.001'7—dc23
                                                                    2015033775

ISBN 978-0-8091-4934-6 (paperback)
ISBN 978-1-58768-523-1 (e-book)

Published by Paulist Press
997 Macarthur Boulevard
Mahwah, New Jersey 07430

www.paulistpress.com

Printed and bound in the
United States of America

CONTENTS

ACKNOWLEDGMENTS

Some of the chapters in this book have appeared elsewhere in Italian or English. All of them have been revised and updated for the present book and are used with permission.

Chapters 1 and 2 originally appeared in *Nello spirito del concilio* (Rome: San Paolo, 2013). Translated by Sean O'Neil.

Chapter 3 was published originally as "The New Elites of Italian Catholicism: 1968 and the New Catholic Movements," *The Catholic Historical Review* 98, no. 1 (January 2012): 18–40.

Chapter 4 was published originally in Italian as "I movimenti cattolici internazionali nel post-concilio: Il caso della recezione del Vaticano II in Italia," in *Da Montini a Martini: Il Vaticano II a Milano. I. Le figure*, ed. Gilles Routhier, Luca Bressan, and Luciano Vaccaro (Brescia: Morcelliana, 2012), 455–71.

Chapter 5's first publication was as "Between Documents and Spirit: The Case of the New Catholic Movements," in *After Vatican II: Trajectories and Hermeneutics*, ed. James L. Heft with John O'Malley (Grand Rapids: Eerdmans, 2012), 1–22. The article was supported by the Institute for Advanced Catholic Studies at the University of Southern California in Los Angeles, directed by James L. Heft.

Chapter 6 appeared originally as "The New Catholic Movements, Vatican II and Freedom in the Catholic Church," *Japan Mission Journal* 62, no. 2 (Summer 2008): 75–84.

PROLOGUE

*T*he *Rising Laity: Ecclesial Movements since Vatican II* is not merely the English translation of parts of the book published in Italy in 2013 under the title of *Nello spirito del concilio. Movimenti ecclesiali e ricezione del Vaticano II.* I have also updated a number of articles published in Europe, Asia, and the United States as well as provided a fresh final chapter on Pope Francis. Taken together, the chapters in this volume are also an expression of my attempt to rethink critically the issue of movements in the Church, focusing on the post–Vatican II period, with particular attention to the global face of these movements and their translation from a European context to that of the United States and the rest of the English-speaking world.

This book about movements is part of a broader effort in my research to combine sociological and political elements of contemporary Catholicism and the institutional dimension in a historical perspective. Despite the postmodern narratives that empower the local, the subjective, and the particular, it is undeniable that in the Roman Catholic Church, the "universal levels" (the Roman Curia, Vatican diplomacy, cosmopolitan Catholic intellectuals) still possess a powerful knowledge structure and intellectual traditions through which they view local circumstances.

Despite Catholic and non-Catholic scholars' attempts, through a wave of "local studies," to portray Catholicism as decentralized, the Catholic Church was (and remains) a centralized institution. In fact, one could argue that over the course of the twentieth century, it has become more centralized than ever before, despite the efforts of the Second Vatican Council (1962–65) to change the structure of church governance. The indifference of scholars of Catholicism to the institutional structures of the Catholic Church is surprising at times. Church historians tend to work less and less on structures and institutions now because church history tends to get lost between theology and ethnography/social history.

The case of the new Catholic movements is a perfect example of the need to combine different methods when we try to understand Catholicism—even more a Catholicism in transition, culturally and geographically, such as the Church of Pope Francis. This book is part of an ongoing work of reflection on this still-developing phenomenon, and most of all, it is part of my ongoing effort to establish better lines of communication between the historical experiences of European and American Catholicism.

Special thanks go to Mark-David Janus, Christopher Bellitto, Bob Byrns, and all the friends at Paulist Press who have believed in my research for all these years.

This book is dedicated to Italy and the Italian Catholicism that gave birth to me. I am still trying to give back from these American shores.

Minneapolis
May 24, 2015, Pentecost Sunday

I

A TRULY CATHOLIC CHURCH

The Institutions and the Movements

T HE GLOBAL NATURE of the Church is an expression of its ability to embrace various forms of Christian life, and it is a historical fact that in the fifty years since Vatican II and what emerged afterward, there has been a period in which we have redefined what it means to be Catholic. On the one hand, there has been a reduction in the traditional indicators of membership (the number of Catholics who go to church either regularly or irregularly; the number of clergy and religious; the impact of social patterns), especially in the West and in Europe. On the other hand, there has been a diversification of the potential models of Christian life within the Catholic Church—far beyond the traditional *duo genera christianorum*, a church divided into "two types of Christian," clergy and laity, with the theologically motivated and sociologically visible assumption of clear superiority of the clergy over the laity.

This impetus toward the laicization and clericalization of the faithful, which was so prevalent in the second millennium, tended to undervalue (if not eliminate) the multiplicity of different forms of Christian life and to push these other forms (such as monastic life, the diaconate, and prophetic voices) in the direction of clericalization.

One can even say that in the imagination of the laity, all religious life assumed a form of "clerical" superiority. This model of church was brought up to date during the twentieth century, and much of this redefinition happened through the birth and development of the "new Catholic movements."

These are a new expression of the element of movement in the Church of the twentieth and twenty-first centuries—after the previous waves of movements in the Church: movements for the poor Church in the eleventh and twelfth centuries and later in the sixteenth century with the new religious orders. But they are also heirs of the movement in the Catholic Church that took place in the late nineteenth and early twentieth century. Particularly from the 1960s and '70s onward, they not only picked up some of the former members of Catholic Action, but also welcomed new types of members, who were marginal rather than mainstream according to the classification designed for the laity by the same Catholic Action during the pontificates of Pius XI and Pius XII. As a result of Vatican II (1962–65), Catholic ecclesiology was updated and redefined, and with it came the redefinition of the role of the laity in the Church.

Nowadays, the "new Catholic movements" are composed of groups like Communion and Liberation, Opus Dei, the Community of Sant'Egidio, the Focolari, the Neocatechumenal Way, the Cursillo, the Regnum Christi movement of the Legionaries of Christ, the Catholic Scouts movement, and other movements that began and grew up within the Catholic Church in the last half-century, and that are active and have a presence beyond the place where they were founded. In Europe, the major movements (and many other less visible movements that are much more difficult to follow) are often presented as the "new vanguard" of Catholicism, the militant and activist wing of a Church struggling to deal with a secular culture.

It is not easy to classify these movements: neither how they define themselves, nor the definitions in the Code of Canon Law and by the magisterium are very helpful. A multidisciplinary approach is indeed required to fully cover the complexities—a historical, theological, canonical, sociological, anthropological approach—and an examination of an area of study that is touched only tangentially by the theological disciplines practiced in the

Catholic Church, that of "new religious movements" (NRM), which is very popular in the English-speaking world.[1]

The basic characteristics that characterize these "new Catholic movements" can be summarized as follows: a group of Catholics with a charismatic founder, a specific charism, some form of expression of communal life or frequent and regular meetings, predominantly lay membership, radical commitment to the gospel, some form of teaching or formation closely linked to its charism, with special attention and commitment paid to bringing its particular charism into the life of the Church. These new movements presuppose a stable commitment and a rule for members to follow, which can be either written or simply part of their way of life. The types of membership (lay, clerical, or mixed) and the lifestyle (celibate, familial, communitarian, monastic, or missionary) vary widely from one movement to the next, and may change within the same movement in different parts of the world.

The life of Catholic movements is indeed like an ever-expanding galaxy and, for now, it is only possible to trace the common and disparate elements in their various expressions. For our attempt to map out current movements—an attempt that is often characterized by a point of view limited by national expressions[2]—we must also add sociological and psychological studies and surveys of the phenomena,[3] in order to try to subdivide the new religious and ecclesial movements into legal, socio-psychological, and political categories. Some attempts to classify them are more successful than others, and it is worth briefly delineating them, drawing on the recent wave of research in Europe, where these movements originated and developed in these last fifty years.

Italian church historian Alberto Melloni has divided them into reform movements, movements of mobilization, and church movements.[4] The French sociologist of religion Danièle Hervieu-Léger has divided them into movements of pilgrims and of converts, with three types of converts: those who change from one religion, which they may or may not have professed actively, to another; those who are converted to the religion from the "irreligious," that is, from a world totally alien to the religious; and those who are "re-affiliated" or "converted from within"—charismatic movements.[5]

Belgian Jesuit and canon lawyer Jean Beyer subdivides them into *lay* movements (made up of members who act among the laity and in the world), *spiritual* movements (which also include religious and diocesan priests), and *ecclesial* movements (the faithful of different states of life who deeply live out the mystery of the Church).[6]

Italian theologian Gianni Ambrosio separates them into movements of *institutional mobilization* (focusing on adapting the missionary aspects of the Church to new patterns in society), *spiritual-emotional mobilization* (which judge modernity to be fragmented, amoral, and for whom only a marginal position in relation to the dominant culture can produce new values: they are attached to the institutional Church, but tend toward the periphery), and the *ascetic-segregative tendency* (the Church must recover its identity through having specific conditions for membership; faithfulness to the Church, making its requirements radical).[7]

An Italian scholar of the new ecclesial communities, Agostino Favale, has classified movements according to their various areas of spiritual and apostolic commitment, Christian animation in the temporal world, Christian inspiration working in the here and now, and more recently, in ecclesial microcommunities (Ecclesial Base Communities, the Neocatechumens), charismatic communities (Charismatic Renewal), neomonastic communities, communities related to movements (Focolarini, communities that have grown out of Communion and Liberation), missionary communities, and communities that are characterized by their openness.[8]

Italian Jesuit Piersandro Vanzan has divided them into movements within the Church whose orientation is spiritual and apostolic (among which are the Focolarini and Ecclesial Base Communities) and movements whose orientation is Christian within the world of today (which include Sant'Egidio communites and Taizé groups).[9]

Movements, if they are real movements, that is, with a low degree of institutional life, are difficult to classify rigidly. But it is clear that the challenge of the movements becomes crucial at the point where the shift in the center of gravity within Catholicism toward the *global south* intersects with Catholicism's shift from Church-as-institution to Church-as-movement. These two trajectories complement each other: Catholicism's European heritage was as a Church-as-state (or as the *establishment*), from its ponderous and costly structures, to its dealings within an increasingly sec-

4

ularized context, while the global future of the Church is destined to move toward national legal contexts in which the Catholic Church does not enjoy tax privileges and political preference, as in Europe, but lives as a minority in a context of a religious and cultural plurality and is therefore likely to be more of a "movement" than an "institution."

This shift presents considerable theological and legal challenges for the Catholic Church, but it also represents an important meeting point for one of the typical phenomena of non-European Christianity, namely that of evangelicalism. These Christians are moved by the missionary spirit that is typical of born-again Protestants, and today it is difficult to evaluate the impact and size of Catholic evangelization in North America, South America, and Africa. But it is also a rapidly growing phenomenon within Catholic dioceses and seminaries, and although it is limited to the confines of "new Catholic movements," it should be seen within this process of redefining global Catholicism.

One of the unknowns of Pope Francis's pontificate—the first to follow the retirement of a pope in modern times—will be the reconfiguration of Rome's role in the universal Church and of the Bishop of Rome's local church as a local church within the universal Church. The reconfiguration of the relationships among the Bishop of Rome, the universal Church, and the Roman local church will have an impact on all of the ecclesial movements, in particular on those that are geographically and historically closer to Rome.

The passing of the pontificate from John Paul II to Benedict XVI in 2005 was not a rupture but, notwithstanding significant reversals on some issues, an extension and an accentuation of some specifically Wojtylian themes: the issue of "continuity" between Benedict XVI and the previous pontificate is relevant not only for the hermeneutics of Vatican II, but also for ecclesial movements and their role within the Church.

The conclave in 2013 was clearly something different than that of 2005 (and probably different than all the conclaves in recent Church history). The cardinals who met in Rome after Benedict XVI's shocking and groundbreaking decision to retire addressed the issue of transparency within the Church, the pedophilia scandal, and the reform of the Roman Curia. If the conclave of 2013

5

updated the Church's public agenda, it did so also because of external pressures. In this new scenario, the role of the movements assumes, if possible, an even greater importance on the Catholic world stage. Pope Francis's ecclesiology of a Church that "goes forth" is in a way an ecclesiology of a Church as a movement. In this sense, my research on the movements, that started in 2003, took a turn in light of Francis's pontificate.

This book contains a historical analysis, but also critical notes on the ecclesiology of the phenomenon of the movements. However, it is *not* an indictment against the "new Catholic movements." It is a book by a historian and theologian that attempts to reconstruct a unified picture of the history of those Catholic movements that, at the end of the twentieth century, spread throughout the world, with sociological and theological characteristics all their own, and whose consequences have still to be assessed at the ecclesiological level. This is one of the reasons why the issue of "new Catholic movements" is not just matter for Europeans and why this book is more than simply a tool for Church historians.

New Catholic movements represent at the same time a contribution to the decentralization and centralization of Catholicism that is still inchoate. The author of this volume is in no way nostalgic for the enthusiasm of the Vatican II era nor for the time before that, but is also convinced that the worldwide Catholic Church cannot turn back: this is the price to be paid at the end of the "age of Constantine" and at the breakup of the very long marriage between Church and state in the West.

It is also clear that the Catholic movements are not only quite different from one another, but also quite different in their cultural and heterogeneous ecclesial contexts within the same movement: Communion and Liberation and the Community of Sant'Egidio in Italy differ in part from Communion and Liberation and Sant'Egidio in North America, especially from the viewpoint of the relationship of adherents to the movement with politics. The same is true of other movements, but this is an issue that deserves to be developed in a different book. However, one of the key elements for understanding the importance of the movements today is just this: the complexity of globalized contemporary Catholicism only appears to be homogeneous.

The theme of movements is also part of the atmosphere of rethinking within the Church about its style of Christianity, which Pope Francis has insisted upon from the beginning of his pontificate, particularly in his homily at the mass of Pentecost, celebrated on May 19, 2013, in St. Peter's Square, which was packed with pilgrims from movements and new communities, associations, and lay groups around the world who came to Rome for the Year of Faith:

> The Holy Spirit would appear to create disorder in the Church, since he brings the diversity of charisms and gifts; yet all this, by his working, is a great source of wealth, for the Holy Spirit is the Spirit of unity, which does not mean uniformity, but which leads everything back to harmony. In the Church, it is the Holy Spirit who creates harmony....Here too, when we are the ones who try to create diversity and close ourselves up in what makes us different and other, we bring division. When we are the ones who want to build unity in accordance with our human plans, we end up creating uniformity, standardization. But if instead we let ourselves be guided by the Spirit, richness, variety and diversity never become a source of conflict, because he impels us to experience variety within the communion of the Church....Having a sense of the Church is something fundamental for every Christian, every community and every movement. It is the Church which brings Christ to me, and me to Christ; parallel journeys are very dangerous![10]

In a church in which it seems necessary to have specific charisms and to advertise "special offers" to the believer in the secularized world, sometimes it seems that the Bible and the liturgy are no longer enough and that the simplicity of living out the gospel has been overwhelmed by increasingly complex and invisible mediation that requires us to live in a plural, multicultural, and multireligious society. If it is true that the movements are an important phenomenon for understanding the attempt by Catholicism to reclaim modernity, to deal with it on their own terms, on the other hand, an ecclesiological reflection on the movements is intended also to rediscover some of the "normal" characteristics of Catholicism, which are part of our shared Christian experience, for Catholics who are part of movements just as for everyone else.

In this sense, the only way to understand the phenomenon of the new Catholic movements is to proceed in different directions from a methodological standpoint: theological, canonical (canon law), sociological, and ethnographical. This book proceeds with two different approaches: vertically, that is, historically, analyzing the steps taken by the Church as an institution in order to deal with the new movements after the watershed of Vatican II; and horizontally, that is, geographically, casting a net in order to try and capture as much as possible the complexity of this phenomenon between its European origins and its global future.

Notes

1. See Massimo Faggioli, "Movimenti religiosi," in *Dizionario del sapere storico-religioso del Novecento*, ed. Alberto Melloni (Bologna: Il Mulino, 2010), 1145–53.

2. There is broad international perspective on the movements in *I movimenti della Chiesa negli anni Ottanta. Atti del Convegno (Roma, 23–27 settembre 1981)*, ed. Massimo Camisasca and Mario Vitali (Milan: Jaca Book, 1982); Bruno Secondin, *I nuovi protagonisti. Movimenti, associazioni, gruppi nella chiesa* (Cinisello Balsamo: Paoline, 1991); Antonio Giolo and Brunetto Salvarani, *I cattolici sono tutti uguali?* (Genoa: Marietti, 1992); Josè Castellano Cervera, *Carismi per il terzo millennio. I movimenti ecclesiali e le nuove comunità* (Rome: OCD, 2001). For a recent contribution on community movements, see Agostino Favale, *Comunità nuove nella chiesa* (Padua: Messaggero, 2003) and *Segni di vitalità nella chiesa. Movimenti e nuove Comunità* (Rome: LAS, 2009).

3. See Giancarlo Quaranta, *L'associazione invisibile. Giovani cattolici tra secolarizzazione e risveglio religioso* (Florence: Sansoni, 1982); Achille Ardigò, Costantino Cipolla, and Stefano Martelli, *Scouts oggi. Diecimila rovers-scolte dell'Agesci rispondono* (Rome: Borla, 1989); Giuseppe Angelini, "I 'movimenti' e l'immagine storica della chiesa. Istruzione di un problema pastorale," *La Scuola Cattolica* 116 (1988): 530–57.

4. See Alberto Melloni, "Movimenti. De significatione verborum," *I movimenti nella Chiesa = Concilium 3*, ed. Alberto Melloni (2003): 13–35. Translated as *Concilium 2003/3 Movements in the Church* (London: SCM Press, 2003).

5. See Danièle Hervieu-Léger, *Le pèlerin et le converti: La religion en mouvement* (Paris: Flammarion, 1999).

6. See Jean Beyer, "De motu ecclesiali quaesita et dubia," *Periodica de re morali canonica liturgica* 78 (1989): 437–52.

7. See Gianni Ambrosio, "Cammino ecclesiale e percorsi aggregative," *La Scuola Cattolica* 116 (1988): 441–60.

8. See Favale, *Comunità nuove nella chiesa*.

9. See Piersandro Vanzan, "Elementi comuni e identificativi dell'attuale fenomeno movimentista intraecclesiale con cenni a rischi e speranze," in *Fedeli Associazioni Movimenti*, ed. Gruppo Italiano di Docenti di Diritto Canonico (Milan: Glossa, 2002), 187–206.

10. Pope Francis, homily at the Holy Mass with the Ecclesial Movements, in St. Peter's Square, May 19, 2013, http://w2.vatican.va/content/francesco/en/homilies/2013/documents/papa-francesco_20130519_omelia-pentecoste.html.

2

Church Movements from Vatican II to John Paul II

THERE ARE FEW ISSUES that polarize observers of and participants in the Church more than the role of movements: members and sponsors of given movements hold differences of opinion, which are often identical but mirrored, when comparing their own movement to its rivals. The evaluation of movements is often unquestioned and undifferentiated and does not take into account the long- and medium-term historical view. In fact, within the broad spectrum of movements, there are instances, sensitivities, and expressions that are quite different than one another: nostalgia for past forms of "Christendom," a push toward ecumenical reform within the Church, a return to clericalism, agencies providing educational and pastoral services, and clear leadership in ecclesiastical contexts. But there is also an acknowledgment that the kind of Christianity that was naturally handed down from generation to generation has ended and an acceptance of the need to recapture the Christian faith and to reformulate how to witness to it in a cultural, social, and political scenario that has profoundly changed over the course of the twentieth century.

This is also why it is necessary to understand the reasons for, and problems with, the extraordinary development of movements during the half-century since Vatican II. Within a few years, movements

11

and ecclesial groups have taken on an extraordinary role and visibility, and not only because of the increase in their numbers, their international expansion, and their skillful strategies for communication, institutionalization, and penetration of the Church hierarchy. Behind this success there are also specific reasons relating to Church politics and a significant shift in papal teaching about them, which often generate tension with the central aspects of the teaching of the Council and its ecclesiology in particular. Rather than carrying out a census and a judgment on individual movements and on the accuracy of the title *movement* for the members of the Church today, we will attempt to summarize the course of their recent development and put forward some suggestions about their "agenda," or about the open problems in the lives of movements within the Church's structure.

VATICAN II AND THE "MOVEMENTS"

One way of looking at Church movements is as fruits, if not *the* fruits par excellence, of Vatican II. In fact, if the break with the previous era marked by the Council is indisputable, then so is the history of these movements, since the experience of Catholic movements has its roots in a previous time dating back to the beginning of the twentieth century. In the decades since the early days of Opus Dei (founded in 1928 in Spain), the mobilization of the Catholic masses by Fr. Riccardo Lombardi, SJ, and the central role of Catholic Action in the "Church of the Piuses" (Pope Pius IX to Pius XII) were in many ways the origin of the contemporary development of ecclesial movements.[1] The Second Vatican Council, called by John XXIII in 1959 and celebrated between 1962 and 1965, occurred after the pontificate of Pius XII had confirmed and lauded the support given to Catholic Action by his predecessor Pius XI. In the wake of developments in the theology of the laity in Europe that, since the late forties, had been focusing on the relationship between the role of the laity, the Church's mission, and its ecclesiology, the Council was historically present at

12

the birth and growth of some Church movements that were then among the most visible and recognized.[2]

But the link between the Council and the movements is more complex than is usually recognized. In fact, the four sessions of Vatican II did not directly address the phenomenon of ecclesial movements, which had not yet manifested themselves with the characteristics of plurality and strength that are so obvious today. The macroissue of Vatican II was ecclesiology, and the debates and the final documents tackled a number of issues related to certain aspects of the life of movements regarding the theology of the laity and the apostolate of the laity, rather than connecting them to the rich experience of the theological and spiritual movements that came prior to the Council: the patristic, liturgical, biblical, and ecumenical movements.[3] In this sense, Vatican II has a lot to say indirectly about the role of the movements in the Church.

Council documents that refer to Church groups, such as the decree *Apostolicam Actuositatem* on the apostolate of the laity, chapter 4 of the constitution *Lumen Gentium* on the laity, paragraph 43 of the pastoral constitution *Gaudium et Spes* on the earthly duties of Christians, and paragraph 8 of the decree *Presbyterorum Ordinis* on associations, constitute a broad base for legitimizing the movements—but only the decree on the apostolate of the laity dealt directly with the issue. In its final stages, the Council debated issues related to the laity, focused on whether to give a more theological orientation to the laity or the need for a precise codification of the laity's rights, duties, and areas of involvement in the Church, while still maintaining an interpretation of the lay apostolate as an expression of the temporal order in communion with the hierarchy.[4]

In chapter 4, "Various Forms of the Apostolate," nos. 18–21 and particularly no. 20, the decree *Apostolicam Actuositatem* tackles questions related to the many different forms of the lay apostolate, the need for the lay apostolate, and the danger of dissipating its forces. No. 20 refers specifically to Catholic Action, presenting it as a typical example of a lay apostolate group, without allowing for other possible types of group, while at the same time hinting at the diversity of groups that might have a variety of purposes, but without recognizing the plurality of ecclesial groups that were then numerically limited and ecclesiastically still more or less underground.[5]

If it is true that the Council documents prepared the ground for subsequent development, or rather subsequent developments can find confirmation in a number of conciliar texts, it should nevertheless be noted that the conciliar texts on the laity are firmly placed within the historical context of the theological view of the laity prior to the Council.[6] The documents of Vatican II on the apostolate should in fact be read again, bearing in mind a dualism in them between hierarchy and laity that will be largely superseded by the development of the postconciliar movements, especially since the early 1980s.[7] The two meetings of the World Congress of the Lay Apostolate in 1951 and 1957 were still marked by the "classic" perspective that in large part also characterized the teaching of Vatican II.[8] This feature ensures that in the teaching of the Council, there is no mention of the element that encourages the faithful to express communion by forming groups. The key point that emerges is that in the Church, the faithful have the right to associate with one another, and this right is exercised in communion with the hierarchy.

Nos. 15–22 of *Apostolicam Actuositatem* describe in magisterial form the historical fact of the "mobilization" of the laity—under the control of the Church hierarchy—as a unique political feature of the twentieth century. Here it is defined theologically, but not canonically—that is, by providing legal forms for this mobilization. From the institutional point of view, the scenario presented to the Council fathers was that of Catholic Action, which was officially and publicly approved and was able—or was believed to be able—to integrate all impulses to form "movements," under the direct control of the papacy and the episcopate.

The Council documents, therefore, have an ecclesiological perspective on the laity that is quite different from the perspective of current Catholic movements during the period of Vatican II's reception at the end of the twentieth century and early twenty-first century. On the one hand, the Council document emphasized the personal nature of the apostolate and the importance of organizations and addressed the missionary aspects of the lay apostolate in a context dominated by Catholic Action. On the other hand, Vatican II opened the way for the multiplicity of ecclesial groups, but with an ecclesiological emphasis on the particular or local (diocesan) church, on the bishop's ministry within the diocese, and on establishing structures for dialogue and coresponsibility of the people of God within local church authorities.

MOVEMENTS DURING THE PONTIFICATE OF PAUL VI (1963–1978)

As helmsman of the crucial stage of the Council, Paul VI remained faithful for a long time to the letter and spirit of Vatican II regarding church groups. Regarding Paul VI's attitude to movements, his long, fifteen-year pontificate can be divided into three periods, according to the emphasis of his teaching on this new reality within the Church:

- A first period of conciliar exegesis (1963–68);
- A second period characterized by prudence and concern regarding the development of ecclesial movements, which was also affected by more general antiestablishment protests (1968–74);
- And a third period, which reestablished the Council teachings and overcame the ecclesiocentrism in relation to Vatican policy toward the movements (1974–78).[9]

The first ten years of Paul VI's pontificate saw the direction of the movements driven more by external events than initiatives within the Church. There was little in the way of pontifical recognition of the movements during the Second Vatican Council: on December 14, 1963, Pope Paul VI approved the Cursillos de Cristiandad,[10] while in 1962, Pope John XXIII had approved *ad experimentum* the Statutes of the General Council of the Opera di Maria–Focolari, which had already been approved in 1957 by the bishop of the diocese of Trent in Northern Italy.[11] In 1964, the Neocatechumenal Way was started on the outskirts of Madrid and arrived at the parish of the Canadian Martyrs in Rome in 1968, along with the founders, Kiko Argüello and Carmen Hernandez.[12]

Between 1968 and 1969, the "Community of Sant'Egidio," founded by the eighteen-year-old layman Andrea Riccardi, took shape in Rome.[13] At the same time, the first "Charismatic Renewal" groups were formed in the United States in the wake of a similar phenomenon that occurred in Protestant circles in the early twentieth century that was even more directly related to the counterculture of the late 1960s. It took root in Italy in 1972.[14]

During the first period after the Council, the bishops and the papacy were rather like spectators at the flowering of the different ecclesial groups, and they studied their development before giving them recognition or disapproval, except in individual cases. During the first decade after the Council, Pope Paul VI's caution and distrust were directed not only to the rebellious and politically progressive choices of some Catholic associations (in Italy, Catholic Action and the Christian Associations of Italian Workers [ACLI]), but also to the "movements" that had proven loyalty toward the hierarchy: Paul VI, as John XXIII had already done before him, refused the requests made in 1960 and in 1962 by the founder Josemaria Escrivá de Balaguer to turn the Opus Dei, founded in Spain in 1928, from a secular institute into a prelature *nullius*.[15]

However, from 1972 to 1973, there were some cautious signs of openness to the new groups that had developed in the very first postconciliar period. In 1972, the publication of the *Ordo initiationis christianae adultorum*—chapter 4 of which suggested that the content of the *Ordo* should be adapted for adults who were baptized but not catechized—conveyed to the leaders of the Neocatechumenal Way a first endorsement. But the Holy See made clear, through the Congregation for Divine Worship and the discipline of the sacraments, that the *Ordo* could apply to anyone who had been baptized. For this reason, the movement adopted the terminology *neocatechumenate*. It received an acknowledgment the following year by the Roman Curia's Congregation for Divine Worship.[16]

Between 1974 and 1975, we can see a change of tack, which was strategic rather than purely tactical, inspired by an assessment of the situation in the Church—and above all by the crisis of Catholic Action—in addition to issues surrounding the reliability of various different movements. During this period, two elements that helped to bring about a turnaround in Paul VI's policy toward movements were the Synod of Bishops in 1974 on evangelization and the apostolic exhortation *Evangelii Nuntiandi* in 1975. In that document, Paul VI considered "apostolic movements" to be still under the heading of *diversified ministries* of the laity, but with a missionary emphasis, and he called them "valuable for the establishment, life, and growth of the Church, and for her capacity to influence her surroundings and to reach those who are remote from her." In fidelity to the coordinating principles of Vatican II, Paul VI also opened the way for a number of ministries in cooperation with the hierarchy, not just for the animation of the temporal order, but also in the service of ecclesial communion: "The laity can also feel themselves called, or be called, to work with their pastors in the service of the ecclesial community for its growth and life, by exercising a great variety of ministries according to the grace and charisms which the Lord is pleased to give them."[17]

But undoubtedly, the attitude toward Communion and Liberation (CL) in Italy also took on significance as one stage of growth in the attitude of the Holy See toward Catholic movements. The movement founded by the Milanese priest Luigi Giussani in 1954 under the name Gioventù Studentesca at this time accomplished the first stage of its historical journey from the margins to the center of the Catholic world.[18] In the early 1970s, CL was one of the few forces in Italian Catholicism that tried to breathe life into an old Catholic movement that was "not uninvolved" in politics: CL was not alone in accepting the invitation of the hierarchy to engage in the campaign against the divorce law in 1974. Having formed the Cattolici Popolari in universities in 1973, in 1975, CL created its political arm, in a dialectical relationship with the Christian Democrats, Movimento Popolare, which held its first public demonstration on November 16, 1975. That was the turning point for the political engagement of CL.

But the turning point from the perspective of the ecclesial visibility of the movement was during the Jubilee of 1975, when CL received a first unofficial recognition by the Vatican; on April 23, 1975, Pope Paul VI put his audience hall at the disposal of the fifteen thousand CL members who had come to Rome to celebrate Holy Year.[19] The following year, in 1976, Communion and Liberation, which had never ceased to arouse suspicion in the highest authorities and was not invited to the national ecclesial Congress, "Evangelization and Human Promotion,"[20] asked the Holy See for approval, but this was granted only in 1981, after the end of Paul VI's pontificate, thanks to John Paul II.[21]

Despite the Vatican's openness, individual bishops had differing opinions, and these bore much weight in the recognition of the various ecclesial groupings and in how they matured into a sense of belonging to the Church. Apart from CL's case, the attitude of the pope and episcopate was much more cautious and aloof toward other movements; the difficulty in obtaining attention and support from the church hierarchy revealed an explicit suspicion of new ecclesial associations. This was true in the case of the Catholic Association of Italian Scouts (AGESCI),[22] whose statutes represented a transition from being a movement to being an association, and were an expression of a deep acceptance of what the Council introduced (evidenced, in Italy just as in France, by the splitting off of the most refractory tendencies into Vatican II and contemporary pedagogical innovations), of an association model, and of a deeply democratic political culture.[23]

It can be said that the attitude of Paul VI toward the movements was essentially accompanied by a magisterial teaching that admitted the historical urgency of the lay apostolic associations and did not rule out forms that were different than Catholic Action. However, Catholic Action, because of its link with the hierarchy, was singled out as the measure and paragon of a lay apostolate group, giving it a privileged place and more individual attention. This teaching, set out within a framework of the increasing difficulty and frustration experienced by the papacy over developments after the Council, gradually took on the tone of concern about the fragmentation of Catholic groups, the loss of cohesion, the anti-institutional spirit that existed, and the lack of a sense of the Church.

The theoretical reflection of Pope Paul VI on the laity and their associations remained faithful to the context of the theology of the laity expressed in the Council documents without making any substantial innovations in terms of ecclesiology and the close bond between the institutional and charismatic elements of this ecclesial reality. The only exception, in the context of Paul VI's prudence regarding the movements, was in the case of CL;

although it seemed more trusting, it was, in reality, still unofficial and wary.

THE DRIVING FORCE BEHIND JOHN PAUL II'S PONTIFICATE (1978–2005)

A turning point in the policy of the Vatican and the papal magisterium with regard to movements arose with the pontificate of John Paul II. From the early years of his pontificate, the thought of John Paul II had been developing. He had been a collaborator with the *Consilium de Laicis*, one of the members of the *Consilium* for the Synod of Bishops who had proposed the theme of evangelization to Paul VI for 1974, and was one of the speakers at that Synod on evangelization. Pope John Paul II's vision of the role of lay groups in the Church in the modern world was expressed often during his apostolic journeys, audiences with the laity, and especially on the Solemnity of Christ the King and in the *ad limina* visits of bishops. Beginning with his programmatic encyclical *Redemptor Hominis* and taking into account the inheritance of the Second Vatican Council and its predecessors, John Paul II observed how a "spirit of collaboration and shared responsibility" could spread even among the laity, "not only strengthening the already existing organizations for lay apostolate but also creating new ones that often have a different outline and excellent dynamism."[24]

The expansion of papal teaching on movements was accompanied by a series of acts and events of extraordinary importance for the future of ecclesial movements.[25] Throughout Pope John Paul II's pontificate, we can identify two main changes in policy toward ecclesial groups: the first consisted in the "launching" of movements in the early years of his pontificate (1981–82), and the second in their being "raised up" during the period of preparation for and celebration of the Jubilee (1998–2000). Since the early years of his pontificate, there had been greater activism: in April 1980, the first conference of movements promoted by the Pontifical Council for the Laity was held; in May 1981, the Italian Bishops' Conference published the report of the Episcopal Commission for the Apostolate of the Laity on the *Criteria for Ecclesiality for Lay Groups, Movements and Associations*;[26] and a few months later, in September 1981, the first international conference of movements was held in Rocca di Papa, organized by Light and Life and Communion and Liberation.[27] On this occasion, which was marked by the contrast inherent in Catholic Action's "religious choice" (close to the culture of progressive "Catholic dissent"), in his brief keynote address, the pope stated that "the Church herself is a movement."[28]

Great attention was given in the early years of the pontificate to Communion and Liberation, which in 1980, in Rimini, celebrated its first *Meeting for Friendship among Peoples* and which in 1982, through its weekly publication *Il Sabato*, proposed that a bishop be appointed who would be responsible for dealing with all the Italian ecclesial movements.[29] In that same year, on February 11, 1982, the Fraternity of Communion and Liberation (founded in 1980 by the Abbot of Monte Cassino with Fr. Giussani as president for life) received from the pope—and not from the Italian Episcopal Conference—recognition as a "lay association of pontifical right," and in September 1982, the pope graced CL with a visit to their meeting in Rimini. The special relationship between John Paul II and Fr. Giussani's movement continued in the following years, until October 1985, when CL was invited, along with other organizations, to participate in the Extraordinary Synod of Bishops, an invitation that was not extended to Catholic Action. This reversal of roles between AC and CL as a model for Italian Catholic movements was one of the major fruits of John Paul's policy for movements in Italy, culminating in the meeting at Loreto in August 2004, in which the "peace" between the two expressions of the Italian laity resulted in a historic change of tack in the pope's preference, to the clear detriment of Catholic Action.

This focus on new movements also involved Opus Dei, which, during the pontificates of John XXIII and Paul VI, had not particularly endeared itself to the Holy See. A redefinition of the external works and activities of Opus Dei followed in the 1970s, aimed at a return to basics—which were educational—and, with the change in pontificate, met with the greatest recognition yet.[30] On November 28, 1982, after a study by the Congregation of Bishops that lasted three and a half years, with the apostolic constitution

Ut Sit Validum, the "Prelature of the Holy Cross and Opus Dei" became a "personal prelature" and Bishop Alvaro del Portillo was appointed as prelate over the organization.

Alongside this activism in favor of movements, the work of reforming the codification of canon law was announced by Pope John XXIII, was moved forward by Paul VI during the 1970s, and was completed in 1983 during the pontificate of John Paul II. However, it did not pay much attention to the canonical aspects of the ecclesial role of charisms and movements. In the 1980 draft of the Code of Canon Law, there were no rules relating to movements, such as were to be found in the draft of *Lex Ecclesiae Fundamentalis*, which, it was thought, would be promulgated soon after. After Pope John Paul II's decision not to publish the *Lex Ecclesiae Fundamentalis*, the rules of canon 15 of *Lex Ecclesiae Fundamentalis* on the rights and duties of the faithful were included in the 1982 draft of the Code of Canon Law, giving rise to canon 215 in the Code of 1983, which is contained in book 2, "De Populo Dei" (part 1, "The Faithful," heading 1, "Rights and Obligations of All the Faithful").

What was suppressed from the draft of 1980 and the final version of 1983 were canon 691, which allowed clerical associations to be incardinated, and canon 307, paragraph 4, on the admission of non-Catholic members into associations.[31] Furthermore, the distinction is made, in canons 298–313 (book 2, "De Populo Dei," part 1 "The Faithful," heading 5, "Associations of the Faithful"), between private and public associations, which comes from civil law.[32] But the Code of 1983 did not want to give a rigid classification of associations, as had the 1917 Code published by Pope Benedict XV. In fact, in contrast with the *personal prelature*—communities of the faithful excluded from the ordinary jurisdiction of bishops, which were included in the Code (c. 294–297)—in the new codification, the term *motus ecclesiales* does not appear; nor was the term *de iure condendo* present, being by definition uncontrollable in law. The same is true of the term *charism*, which is mentioned seven times in the draft of 1982, then deleted and absent from the final text.[33]

During the 1980s, the growth of movements and associations in the light of the papal policy was consistent and full of significant events and position statements, even by close associates of John Paul II: in his *Report on the Faith*, the prefect of the Congregation for the Doctrine of the Faith, Cardinal Joseph Ratzinger, said that the intense life of faith within the movements was not to be understood as a way of escaping into a private devotion or a backward step, but a "full and complete Catholicism," and the Church had a duty to make room for them.[34] Even the frequent apostolic trips of his pontificate and the start of World Youth Day, which had occured every three years since 1984 and then every two years, offered a prominent stage to the ecclesial movements, which were able to focus on the pope of Rome as the legitimizing reference point for ecclesial movements, which often had strained relations, when not in direct conflict, with the local hierarchy, bishops, and bishops' conferences. The first major event that connected the "new movements" to the call to young people in the Church was in 1984 in Rome, during the Jubilee of the Redemption 1983–84, in which Communion and Liberation had a specific role.

At the second Conference of the Italian Church in Loreto, in April 1985, the pope called the movements "the channel for the formation and promotion of a laity that was active and aware of its role in the church and in the world," and indicated that what was essential was the "'necessary' and 'constant' reference to one's bishop."[35] At the second meeting of the movements at Rocca di Papa, in February–March 1987, John Paul II said that "the great flowering of these movements and the manifestations of energy and vitality that characterize the Church are to be considered certainly one of the finest fruits of the vast and profound spiritual renewal promoted by the last Council."[36]

The growth of their influence, however, was not shared equally by all the pastors of the local churches. At the 1987 Synod on the Laity—at which many representatives of the movements of various countries took part as observers—some senior members of the hierarchy expressed opinions that were problematic: Cardinals Martini, Lorscheider, and Tomasek spoke of the movements as "parallel churches."[37] But the overall result of the Synod did not seem to take into account the concerns raised in relation to the ecclesiology of movements and the pastoral problems related to their activities in dioceses and parishes. The postsynodal apostolic exhortation *Christifideles Laici*, published January 30, 1989, defined the group apostolate as "a 'sign' that must be manifested in relation to 'communion' both in the internal and external aspects of the various group forms and in the wider context of the Christian community." This sign was linked to the signs of the times:

> In recent days the phenomenon of lay people associating among themselves has taken on a character of particular variety and vitality. In some ways lay associations have always been present throughout the Church's history as various confraternities, third orders and sodalities testify even today. However, in modern times such lay groups have received a special stimulus, resulting in the birth and spread of a multiplicity of group forms: associations, groups, communities, movements. We can speak of a new era of group endeavours of the lay faithful.[38]

The pope adopted a perspective that largely took note of the existing reality and pointed out the five criteria for ecclesiality: (1) the primacy given to the call of every Christian to holiness; (2) responsibility of professing the Catholic faith; (3) the witness to a strong and authentic communion; (4) conformity to and participation in the Church's apostolic goals; (5) commitment to a presence in human society.[39]

The presence of the theme of movements in the Church's teaching never faded over the course of the nineties, when it became increasingly clear that John Paul II saw in the movements specialized and more advanced implementers of the "new evangelization." Beside this role, the internal development of the church movements posed some questions of coexistence with the traditional structures for the recruitment and training of the clergy. Even the declaration of the Extraordinary Synod of Bishops for Europe in 1991 and the following postsynodal apostolic exhortation *Pastores Dabo Vobis* in 1992 faced the problem of the new characteristics of the priests in their movements, emphasizing the positive role of these new groups in the pastoral care of vocations, and gave positive value to the link between the seminarians and priests and the groups from which they came:

> Associations and youth movements, which are a sign and confirmation of the vitality which the Spirit guarantees

to the Church, can and should contribute also to the formation of candidates for the priesthood, in particular of those who are the product of the Christian, spiritual and apostolic experience of these groups. Young people who have received their basic formation in such groups and look to them for their experience of the Church should not feel they are being asked to uproot themselves from their past or to break their links with the environment which has contributed to their decision to respond to their vocation, nor should they erase the characteristic traits of the spirituality which they have learned and lived there in all that they contain that is good, edifying and rich. For them too, this environment from which they come continues to be a source of help and support on the path of formation toward the priesthood.[40]

In 1993, the pastoral letter of the Episcopal Commission of the Italian Episcopal Conference for the Laity, called *Lay Groups in the Church*, signified a substantial openness to the movements, a direct acceptance of no. 41 of *Christifideles Laici* on the development of the five principles of ecclesiality, but also a warning to the movements not to consider themselves to be *the* Church.[41] The role of the movements in the new evangelization was also mentioned in the letter *Tertio Millennio Adveniente*, in which, among the signs of hope for the new evangelization, the pope emphasized, "In the Church, they include a greater attention to the voice of the Spirit through the acceptance of charisms and the promotion of the laity."[42]

Similarly, in the postsynodal apostolic exhortation *Vita Consecrata* in 1996, John Paul II remarked on the role of movements in more problematic terms in relation to the participation of consecrated persons in ecclesial movements:

In recent years, many consecrated persons have become members of one or other of the ecclesial movements which have spread in our time. From these experiences, those involved usually draw benefit, especially in the area of spiritual renewal. Nonetheless, it cannot be denied that in certain cases this involvement causes uneasiness and disorientation at the personal or community level, especially when these experiences come into conflict with the demands of the common life or of the Institute's spirituality. It is therefore necessary to take care that membership in these ecclesial movements does not endanger the charism or discipline of the Institute of origin, and that all is done with the permission of Superiors and with the full intention of accepting their decisions.[43]

The policy of recognizing the movements grew significantly during the nineties, up to the final step of the preparation and management of the Jubilee of 2000. In May 1998, the Fourth World Congress of the movements and new communities[44] was held in Rome. About three hundred thousand members of sixty movements and new communities were welcomed by the pope, who in his speech on the eve of Pentecost (May 27, 1998), called them "the answer" to the challenge of secularization: in that speech, the movements were described as "one of the most significant fruits of that springtime in the Church which was foretold by the Second Vatican Council, but unfortunately has often been hampered by the spread of secularization."[45] The pope also showed an open agenda regarding the path of movement along the road to "ecclesial maturity," calling the movements again to offer to the church "'mature' fruits of communion and commitment."[46]

An even clearer sign of favor toward the movements came from Cardinal Ratzinger in his address to the Fourth Congress in 1998. The future Benedict XVI placed the ecclesial movements beyond an ambiguous "dialectic of principles" (such as charisma/institution, Christology/pneumatology, hierarchy/prophecy) and saw them instead as a response of the Spirit for cooperation in its universal apostolate and strongly distanced himself from the criticism of diocesan bishops against some movements and their exclusivist nature. Ratzinger gave the movements a timely reminder—to be faithful to the totality of the Church and submit to the requirements of this totality—and he had four reminders for local churches and bishops: (1) it is not possible for them to expect uniformity within organizations and pastoral planning; (2) it is not for them to say what the Spirit can do and not do; (3) they cannot require a concept of communion that is merely intended to avoid conflict; (4) they cannot label "the zeal of people animated by the Holy Spirit and their candid faith in the Word of God as fundamentalist."[47]

In June 1999, it was the turn of the International Conference in Speyer, "For Communion between Movements and New Communities," promoted by the Charismatic Renewal, the Community of Sant'Egidio, and the Focolare. In June 2001, in Castel Gandolfo, the 10th Congress of Pastoral Theology was held, the subject of which was "Movements for the New Evangelization," with the participation of the Community of Sant'Egidio, Chiara Lubich for the Focolare, the Neocatechumenal Way, Communion and Liberation, many Vatican authorities, and 1,300 priests belonging to various movements.

The occurrence of the Jubilee of the Year 2000 also brought with it recognition and consecration for the life of the individual movements. This was not particularly problematic because of the support offered to Opus Dei by John Paul II from the beginning of his pontificate, but there was further recognition given to the prelature with the canonization of founder Josemaría Escrivá de Balaguer on October 6, 2002 (after his beatification in 1992), while in other cases the transition of the Jubilee consisted of a special "indulgence" even for movements that had been under scrutiny for a long time or had fallen into temporary disfavor. At its meeting from September 20 to 23, 1999, the Italian Bishops' Conference approved the Statute of the Cursillo Movement; similarly, for the Neocatechumenal Way, after first steps in the early nineties,[48] the new millennium brought *ad experimentum* approval for five years of *Statute of the Neocatechumenal Way*, which was published on June 29, 2002.[49] On March 14, 2002, Charismatic Renewal, on the thirtieth anniversary of its presence in the Italian church, received confirmation of the statutes of the association from the Italian Episcopal Conference.[50]

The death of Fr. Luigi Giussani occurred in February 2005, just weeks before the death of John Paul II. The homily given by Cardinal Ratzinger at the funeral of Giussani in Milan symbolically summed up the importance of the role of CL in the pontificate of the Polish pope. But a few weeks after the conclave, in

April 2005, there was also a sign of continuity in Vatican policy on movements, in the complex relationship between the direction given to the Church during the twenty-seven years of John Paul II's papacy and the direction of his successor. The death of "the pope of movements" on April 2, 2005, and the election of Benedict XVI—who for twenty-three years had been the main architect of John Paul II's doctrinal policies—on April 19, 2005, reassured the movements about the continuity (one of the mantras of Ratzinger's theological following) of the papacy's attitude toward this new phenomenon. The election to the papacy of the archbishop of Milan, Cardinal Carlo Maria Martini, SJ, who was very critical of the movements at the synod of 1987 (as well as other times), would have caused the leadership of these important new realities in the Church many more worries.

This continuity between John Paul II and Benedict XVI in the Vatican's attitude toward new ecclesial movements had important consequences not only at the theological level, but also at the level of the configuration of the lay elites (real or self-attributed elites will be covered in another chapter) of the new global Catholicism. This was especially true in a country like Italy that has been and still is an influential model (or for some, antimodel) for the rest of world Catholicism.

Notes

1. For a brief history of the individual movements, see Agostino Favale, *Movimenti ecclesiali contemporanei. Dimensioni storiche, teologico-spirituali ed apostoliche* (Rome: LAS, 1982, 1991). On the history of Catholic Action, see Mario Casella, *L'Azione cattolica alla caduta del fascismo: Attività e progetti per il dopoguerra, 1942–45* (Rome: Studium, 1984), and "L'Azione Cattolica del tempo di Pio XI e di Pio XII (1922–1958)," in *Dizionario Storico del Movimento Cattolico in Italia (1860–1980)*, vol. 1 (Turin: Marietti, 1981), 1, 84–101; on the role of the Catholic Action in Italy as a model, see John Pollard, "Pius XI's Promotion of the Italian Model of Catholic Action in the World-Wide Church," *The Journal of Ecclesiastical History* 63, no. 4 (2012): 758–84.

2. Among others, see Yves Congar, *Jalons pour une théologie du laïcat* (Paris: Cerf, 1953); Gustave Thils, *Théologie des réalités terrestres* (Bruges: De Brouwer, 1947–49); Joseph Cardijn, *Laïcs en premières lignes* (Paris: Éditions Universitaires, 1963).

3. See Étienne Fouilloux, "'Mouvements' théologico-spirituels et concile (1959–1962)," in *À la veille du Concile Vatican II. Vota et réactions en Europe et dans le catholicisme oriental,* ed. Mathijs Lamberigts and Claude Soetens (Leuven: Bibliotheek van de Faculteit der Godgeleerdheid, 1992), 185–99.

4. See *Storia del concilio Vaticano II,* vol. 4 of *La chiesa come comunione,* ed. Giuseppe Alberigo (Bologna: Il Mulino, 1999), 259–91.

5. See Barbara Zadra, *I movimenti ecclesiali e i loro statuti* (Rome: Pontificia Università Gregoriana, 1997), 7–21.

6. See Franco Giulio Brambilla, "Le aggregazioni ecclesiali nei documenti del magistero dal concilio fino ad oggi," *La Scuola Cattolica* 116 (1988): 461–511, at 474. More recently, Brendan Leahy, *Ecclesial Movements and Communities: Origins, Significance, and Issues* (Hyde Park, NY: New City Press, 2011).

7. See Bruno Forte, "Associazioni, movimenti e missione nella chiesa locale," *Il Regno-Documenti* 1 (1983): 29–34. For an overview of the issues arising from the canonically mixed composition (laity, clergy, single, married) of many movements and new ecclesial communities, cf. Juan José Etxeberría, "Los movimientos eclesiales en los albores del siglo XXI," *Revista Española de Derecho Canonico* 58 (2001): 577–616.

8. See Bernard Minvielle, *L'apostolat des laïcs à la veille du Concile (1949–1959). Histoire des congrès mondiaux de 1951 et 1957* (Fribourg: Éditions universitaires, 2001). For the subsequent period, see Ludovic Laloux, "Les étapes du renouvellement de l'apostolat des laïcs en France depuis le Concile Vatican II" (unpublished thesis, Université de Lille, 1999), from which "L'apostolat des laïcs en France. D'une politique hexagonale aux impulsions romaines," *Nouvelle Revue Théologique* 122 (2000): 211–37.

9. See Brambilla, "Le aggregazioni ecclesiali nei documenti del magistero," 491–504, especially 478–91. Paul VI's vision for the movements does not appear in Renato Marangoni's *La chiesa mistero di comunione. Il contributo di Paolo VI nell'elaborazione dell'ecclesiologia di comunione (1963–1978)* (Rome: Gregorian Pontifical University, 2001).

10. The movement was formed in Spain at the end of the forties within Catholic Action, and spread outside of Spain from 1953: on its official approval, see *Acta Apostolicae Sedis* 56 (1964): 524–25; Favale, *Movimenti ecclesiali contemporanei.*

11. The Statutes were approved in 1962, and the seventh edition was published in 1964: cf. *Statuti generali dell'Opera di Maria* (Rome: typography Mariapoli, 1964). See Christoph Hegge, *Il Vaticano II e i movimenti ecclesiali. Una recezione carismatica* (Rome: Città Nuova, 2001), 168.

12. See Antonio Giolo and Brunetto Salvarani, *I cattolici sono tutti*

uguali? Una mappa dei movimenti della Chiesa (Genova: Marietti, 1992). One of the rare writings by Kiko Argüello, "Le comunità neocatecumenali," *Rivista di vita spirituale* 2 (1975): 191–92. See also Argüello, *Il kerigma. Nelle baracche con i poveri* (Cinisello Balsamo: San Paolo, 2013).

13. See Andrea Riccardi, *Sant'Egidio, Rome et le monde. Entretiens avec Jean-Dominique Durand et Regis Ladous* (Paris: Beauchesne, 1996). Translated by Peter Heinegg as *Sant' Egidio, Rome, and the World* (London: St. Pauls, 1999).

14. See Enzo Pace, "Le possibili basi del fondamentalismo cattolico contemporaneo," in *Ai quattro angoli del fondamentalismo. Movimenti politicoreligiosi nella loro tradizione, epifania, protesta, regressione,* ed. Roberto Giammanco (Scandicci: La Nuova Italia, 1993), 351–415.

15. See Ambrosio, "Cammino ecclesiale e percorsi aggregative," 441–60.

16. See Pietro Sorci, "Ermeneutica della Parola nel cammino neocatecumenale," *Rivista liturgica* 84, no. 6 (1997): 867–80.

17. Paul VI, apostolic exhortation *Evangelii Nuntiandi,* December 8, 1975, no. 73.

18. See Salvatore Abbruzzese, *Comunione e Liberazione. Identité catholique et disqualification du monde* (Paris: Cerf, 1989) and, for a recent synthesis by the same author, *Comunione e Liberazione* (Bologna: Il Mulino, 2001). For an inside and official history of the origins of Communion and Liberation, see Massimo Camisasca, *Comunione e Liberazione. Le origini (1954–1968)* (Cinisello Balsamo: Paoline, 2001) and *Comunione e Liberazione. La ripresa (1969-1976)* (Cinisello Balsamo: Paoline, 2003). For a study on the theology and anthropology of Communion and Liberation, see Anke M. Dadder, *Comunione e Liberazione. Phänomenologie einer neuen geistlichen Bewegung* (Constance: UVK, 2002), esp. 97–142.

19. See Camisasca, *Comunione e Liberazione. La ripresa,* 287–316. About the complex relationship between CL and the political culture of extremist fringes of "Catholic dissent" involved in domestic terrorism in 1970s Italy, see Guido Panvini, *Cattolici e violenza politica. L'altro album di famiglia del terrorismo italiano* (Venice: Marsilio, 2014), esp. 364–68.

20. On the subject of Paul VI's and the Italian bishops' caution toward Communion and Liberation, see Massimo Faggioli, "Tra referendum sul divorzio e revisione del Concordato. Enrico Bartoletti segretario della CEI (1972–1976)," *Contemporanea* 2 (2001): 255–80. The absence of an invitation to Communion and Liberation was motivated by the fact that Communion and Liberation, unlike other invited movements, was not recognized by the Italian Episcopal Conference (CEI) and was not part of the Council for the Lay Apostolate (Communion and Liberation

would join the CEI's Council of Lay Associations in 1991); no less hard was the reaction of Communion and Liberation, which felt that they were implicated by the report to the conference by one of the organizers, Fr. Bartolomeo Sorge, SJ, and his reference to the "rot of integralism."

21. Communion and Liberation's first requests to the Italian bishops for a statute came in 1972.

22. AGESCI, the Association of Italian Catholic Guides and Scouts, founded in 1974 by the merger of the ASCI Association for boys and the AGI association for girls, was recognized by the IEC only after much pressure in 1978. Between 1974 and 1975, meetings between the secretary of CEI and Paul VI, and within the CEI, revealed the concerns of the hierarchy over their coming together and the potential for promiscuity between the sexes by choosing coeducation, over the role of the priest as church assistant, and on the infiltration of Marxist ideology identified in the antifascist stance present in the charter of the association; see the minutes of the audience of Bishop Enrico Bartoletti (secretary general of the Italian bishops' conference) with Paul VI, July 10, 1975. See Mario Sica, *Storia dello scoutismo in Italia* (Scandicci: La Nuova Italia, 1973), which was reissued several times until its 2007 edition through Fiordaliso, Rome. On this, see Massimo Faggioli, "The New Elites of Italian Catholicism: 1968 and the New Catholic Movements," *The Catholic Historical Review* 98, no. 1 (2012): 18–40, and "I movimenti cattolici internazionali nel post-concilio: il caso della recezione del Vaticano II in Italia," in *Da Montini a Martini: il Vaticano II a Milano. I. Le figure*, ed. Gilles Routhier, Luca Bressan, and Luciano Vaccaro (Brescia: Morcelliana, 2012), 455–71.

23. See Philippe Laneyrie, *Les Scouts de France. L'évolution du Mouvement des origines aux années 80* (Paris: Cerf, 1985), esp. 325–26.

24. John Paul II, encyclical *Redemptor Hominis*, March 4, 1979, no. 5.

25. See Brambilla, "Le aggregazioni ecclesiali nei documenti del magistero," especially 491–504.

26. See *Enchiridion della Conferenza episcopale italiana*, 3 (1980–85) (Bologna: EDB, 1986), 309–30.

27. See *I movimenti della Chiesa negli anni Ottanta. Atti del Convegno (Roma, 23–27 settembre 1981)*, ed. Massimo Camisasca and Mario Vitali (Milan: Jaca Book, 1982). Other meetings were held from February 28 to March 4, 1987 in Rocca di Papa (see *I movimenti nella Chiesa. Atti del II colloquio internazionale. Vocazione e missione dei laici nella chiesa oggi* [Milan: Nuovo Mondo, 1987]), from April 1 to 4, 1991, at Bratislava, and for Pentecost 1998 in Rome.

28. Homily of September 27, 1981, in *Insegnamenti di Giovanni Paolo II*, vol. 4, no. 2 (Vatican City: LEV, 1982), 305.

29. Cf. "Un vescovo per i movimenti?" *Il Regno* 22 (1982): 507.

30. See Pace, "Le possibili basi del fondamentalismo cattolico contemporaneo," 395–96.

31. See Zadra, *I movimenti ecclesiali e i loro statuti*, and Velasio De Paolis, "Diritto dei fedeli di associarsi e la normativa che lo regola," in *Fedeli Associazioni Movimenti*, ed. Gruppo Italiano di Docenti di Diritto Canonico (Milan: Glossa, 2002), 127–62.

32. See Ludger Müller, "Das Kirchliche Vereinigungsrecht im CIC/1983. Ekklesiologische Grundlage und kirchenrechtliche Neuordnung," *Osterreichisches Archiv für Kirchenrecht* 36 (1986): 293–305.

33. "While Vatican II deeply appreciates the variety and multiplicity of forms of association…, the Code of Canon Law for the Latin Rite (CIC) does not hesitate to encapsulate and standardize them all, in the wake of the CIC in 1917, within the traditional corporatist model, without taking into account the peculiarities of communal forms of apostolate that thrive in the contemporary church, such as movements, societies, grassroots communities (which are recognized not only by the documents of Medellin and Puebla, but also by *Evangelii Nuntiandi*), and which refuse, because of their spiritual identity, to be subsumed under the legal concept of association or, if having to accept the classification, adopt it as formal legal superstructure without any real content and make it, therefore, ultimately foreign to them": Eugenio Corecco, "Aspetti della recezione del Vaticano II nel codice di diritto canonico," in *Il Vaticano II e la chiesa*, ed. Giuseppe Alberigo and Jean-Pierre Jossua (Brescia: Paideia, 1985), 333–97, at 360; see also E. Corecco, "Die kulturellen und ekklesiologischen Vo riraussetzungen des neuen CIC," *Archiv für katholisches Kirchenrecht* 152 (1983): 3–30; "Profili istituzionali dei movimenti nella Chiesa," in ibid., *Ius et Communio. Scritti di diritto canonico* vol. 2 (Lugano: Faculty of Theology di Lugano, 1997), 143–74; Libero Gerosa, "Carismi e movimenti ecclesiali: una sfida per la canonistica postconciliare," *Periodica* 82, no. 3 (1993): 411–30.

34. See Joseph Ratzinger with Vittorio Messori, *Rapporto sulla fede* (Milan: Paoline, 1985), 42–43. Translated by Graham Harrison as *The Ratzinger Report: An Exclusive Interview on the State of the Church* (San Francisco: Ignatius Press, 1986).

35. See Paolo Urso, "Alcune problematiche fra movimenti e chiesa particolare, ministero ordinato e celebrazione eucaristica," in Gruppo Italiano di Docenti di Diritto Canonico, *Fedeli Associazioni Movimenti*, 231–53.

36. Address given on March 2, 1987, *Insegnamenti* 10, no. 1 (1987): 476.

37. See Giuseppe Caprile, ed., *Il Sinodo dei Vescovi. Settima assemblea generale ordinaria (1–30 ottobre 1987)* (Rome: La Civiltà Cattolica,

1989). See Giolo and Salvarani, *I cattolici sono tutti uguali? Una mappa dei movimenti della Chiesa*; see Jesús Bogarín Diaz, "Los movimientos eclesiales en la VII Asamblea General Ordinaria del Sinodo de Obispos," *Revista española de Derecho Canónico* 47 (1990): 69–135. Cardinal Carlo Maria Martini returned to the theme of the parish/movement dualism during the Synod of Bishops on Europe in 1999 (in *Il Regno-Documenti* 19 [1999]: 608).

38. John Paul II, postsynodal apostolic exhortation *Christifedeles Laici*, December 30, 1988, no. 29.

39. Ibid., nos. 30 and 46–47.

40. Postsynodal apostolic exhortation *Pastores Dabo Vobis*, March 25, 1992, no. 68.

41. Episcopal Commission of the Italian Episcopal Conference for the Laity, "Le aggregazioni laicali nella Chiesa," April 29, 1993, in *Enchiridion della Conferenza episcopale italiana: decreti, dichiarazioni, documenti pastorali per la Chiesa italiana* vol. 5 (1991–1995) (Bologna: EDB, 1996), 697–739. The letter makes the distinction between associations, movements, and groups on the basis of decreasing institutional structure (membership mechanisms, governance functions).

42. John Paul II, apostolic letter *Tertio Millenio Adveniente*, November 10, 1994, nos. 46–47.

43. John Paul II, postsynodal apostolic exhortation *Vita Consecrata*, March 25, 1996, no. 56.

44. The most notable movements of who were present at the Congress in 1998: the Neocatechumenal Way, Communauté de l'Arche, the Communauté de l'Emmanuel, Communion and Liberation, the Community of Sant'Egidio, Cursillos, the Foyers de Charité, Legion of Mary, the Focolare Movement (Opera di Maria), Schoenstatt, Charismatic Renewal.

45. *I movimenti nella chiesa. Atti del convegno mondiale dei movimenti ecclesiali (Roma 27-29 maggio 1998)* (Vatican City: LEV, 1999); for the pope's speech on May 27, 1998, see http://www.vatican.va/holy_father/ john_paul_ii/speeches/1998/may/documents/hf_jp-ii_spe_19980527_ movimenti_en.html. See also *I Movimenti ecclesiali nella sollecitudine pastorale dei Vescovi* (Vatican City: LEV, 2000); and the Pontifical Council for the Laity, *Il Papa e i movimenti. Testi e immagini dell'incontro del Santo Padre con i Movimenti ecclesiali e le Nuove Comunità* (Cinisello Balsamo: San Paolo, 1998).

46. Address of John Paul II to the IV World Congress of Ecclesial Movements, May 30, 1998, http://www.vatican.va/holy_father/john_

paul_ii/speeches/1998/may/documents/hf_jp-ii_spe_19980530_rifles
sioni_en.html.

47. See Joseph Ratzinger, "I movimenti ecclesiali e la loro collo-cazione teologica," in *I movimenti nella chiesa*, 23–51, and in *Il Regno-Documenti* 13 (1998): 399–406.

48. In August 30, 1990, the pope recognized the Neocatechu-menal Way as "an effective means of Catholic formation for society and for the present time." See *Acta Apostolicae Sedis* 82 (1990): 1513–15, https://w2.vatican.va/content/john-paul-ii/en/letters/1990/documents/hf_jp-ii_let_19900830_ogni-qualvolta.html.

49. During the audience with the founders and leaders on January 24, 1997, on the thirtieth anniversary of the founding of the Way, the pope had asked for a statute, the preparation of which began with a pilgrimage to Sinai. After that, in 2001, there had been a solicitation of the pope to Cardinal James Francis Stafford for the Pontifical Council for the Laity to come to a final judgment on the Way (April 2001) and a letter of request to have a constitution.

50. See Lorenzo Prezzi, "Statuti definitivi," *Il Regno-Attualità* 8 (2002): 240.

3

RELIGION AND POLITICS OF THE NEW ECCLESIAL MOVEMENTS

The Sixties and the New Elites of Italian Catholicism

T HE POST–VATICAN II period saw the rise of the new Catholic movements within the Catholic Church. In Italy, this phenomenon crossed paths with the sixties and, in particular, with the year 1968, the peak of the students' protests, with young Catholics playing an important role. This confluence of theological renewal and sociopolitical protests meant the creation of a new elite not only in the Catholic Church worldwide, but especially in Italian Catholicism. The ways these movements reacted to and participated in 1968 in Italy were extremely different and marked the development of a deeply rooted diversity within Italian Catholicism. Besides their differences, the Catholic movements were an initial step in the ongoing process of the replacement of old clerical elites in Catholic Europe.

A FATHERLESS CHILD IN THE MEMORY OF ITALIAN CHURCH AND POLITICS: 1968 AND THE SIXTIES

The public debate on the role of Catholicism in Italy's recent history is split into two very different and, in many respects, opposite ways of looking at the subject. Most interpreters of the history of the relationship between Italian Catholicism and the post-1968 cultural and political landscape tend to describe the directions taken by Italian Catholics in two ways: on one side, there is liberal/progressive "Vatican II Catholicism" allied with radical/revolutionary leftists, and on another side, there is "conservative Catholicism" supporting right-wing, post–Cold War Italian political parties. This story of the recent past of Italian Catholicism is clearly part of an ideological narrative that supported Silvio Berlusconi's two decades of political supremacy in Italy, beginning in 1994. However, the political-cultural contribution of the sixties to the culture of the Catholic Church is much more complex. The series of events evoked by 1968 played a major role in Italy, by polarizing the new cultural impulses of the 1960s, stopping the successful experiments of the early 1960s, and halting a much-needed turnover of the elites. That is true for the social and political history of Italy as well as for the history of Italian Catholicism.

The complexity of the ideological and cultural rifts in the 1960s, especially in the period between the end of Vatican II in 1965 and the first crisis of the post–Vatican II era between 1968 and 1970 (due to Hans Küng's book *The Church*,[1] the *Dutch Catechism*,[2] and Paul VI's encyclical *Humanae Vitae* and its reception) still requires much analysis. This analysis must include the role of the Catholic movements in Italy.

This rift around the interpretation of the role of Catholicism in Italy in the 1960s and 1970s reflects a deep cultural deficiency in the analysis of the social and political role of Catholicism in twentieth-century Italy. This is partly because critics of the political role of Catholicism in Italy follow the very traditional concept of the Catholic Church as a vertical institution ruled by the pope and Roman Curia, cardinals, bishops, and clergy. Alternatively, many view the renewed public presence of Catholicism purely as a right-wing Catholic revanche. Both ways of seeing the Church as a social and political player are somehow still true and complementary, but they show traces of a sociological approach to Catholicism that still needs to be completed with a historical approach, especially considering the new faces of the so-called new Catholic movements and their role in the creation of a new Italian Catholic "leading elite."[3] The picture should be examined from a historical point of view that aims to study the historical development of Italian Catholicism and its peculiar features, characters, and culture. Assessing the recent history of Italian Catholicism means taking into account a new category of protagonists, whose arrival on the stage has been underestimated by historians of modern Italian Catholicism and overestimated by sociologists of religion and forecasters of the "postsecular age" in Italy.

This chapter will attempt to underline the role of the new Catholic movements and their rise in the period between the end of Vatican II and the 1970s in the political, ideological, and sociological framework of present-day Catholicism in Italy. This approach will offer, on the one hand, a more nuanced view of the social and political aggiornamento of Italian Catholicism and the opportunity to reassess the often-overlooked changing political-cultural identity of the Italian church between two key dates in the period between Vatican II and today: the year of the students' protests in 1968, and the end of the Cold War in Europe between 1989 and 1991. On the other hand, it will become clear that a large part of the contemporary Italian Catholic elite and of Catholic lay movements derives from Italian Catholics' endeavor to make sense and come to terms with the difficult ideological divide in Italy during the "tumultuous 1960s." In fact, the example of the Catholic movements and the events of 1968 in Italy shows that the relationship between the reception of Vatican II, "Catholic radicalism," and the ideological clash in Italy is much more intricate than it is usually portrayed. If we looked at the bending of the arc of the ideological history of the new Catholic movements between 1968 and the beginning of the twenty-first century, we would draw surprising conclusions.

CATHOLICISM AND 1968 IN ITALY: A SHIFT IN THE HISTORY OF CATHOLIC MOVEMENTS

The official historiography of the new Catholic movements tends to stress, uncritically and apologetically, the coincidence of their dates of birth with Vatican II, but their relationship to the events of 1968 and the sociopolitical meaning of that period is much more important, ambivalent, and unexplored than we may think. The year 1968 in Catholicism must be framed in a complex context, between Vatican Council II and the 1970s, on the one hand, and between the end of the "long nineteenth century"[4] and the peak of a thorough secularization of Europe, on the other. Such a periodization intends to see 1968's Catholicism in a global context, immediately after the most globalized event in the history of the Catholic Church—Vatican II.[5]

The pontificate of Paul VI played a significant role in the history of the relations between the Church and the modern world, and also *within the Church* between lay movements and the ecclesiastical institution. We cannot diminish the importance of the change in the balance of power within the Catholic Church. Vatican II meant not only a debate between theologies and social and political cultures, but also a turnover in the balances of power in an institution deeply marked by a stratification in the social identity of power holders: bishops, clergy, monks, religious orders, and Catholic nobility.[6]

The social dynamics of Catholics after Vatican II was symbolized by Paul VI, who prepared a massive turnover in the elite of the Church, thanks to new regulations that "invited" bishops to resign their office when they turned seventy-five.[7] This decision changed the face of the Italian episcopate almost overnight, but the social dynamics of the post–Vatican II Catholic Church went much deeper and further. It is beyond doubt that the 1968 movements received some input from post–Vatican II Catholicism, maybe more than has been acknowledged, and much more in Europe (Italy, France, Germany) than in North America.[8] Italy played a special role in the attempt to link the struggle for

Vatican II with the 1968 movements, while assessing the effects of 1968 on the Catholic Church as an institution.

The role of Italian Catholics in the 1968 movement has been studied and judged in different ways. On the protests at the Catholic University in Milan, the real beginning of 1968 in Italy, Italian historian Agostino Giovagnoli stated, "It would be an overstatement to say that the religious element played a decisive role."[9] But Salvatore Abbruzzese more convincingly affirmed in his classic study on Communion and Liberation, "This presence of Catholics within the movement of 1968 was less marginal than we might suppose."[10]

The struggle for the reception/application of Vatican II met the political climate of the sixties and offered the opportunity for a more general attempt to renovate, not just the language, symbolism, or theology of Catholicism, but even the leading elites of the Church as an institution. The new conciliar weltanschauung implied disposing of an old religious elite and replacing it with a new one. In the memories of 1968 as catastrophe evoked by conservative Catholics at the beginning of the twenty-first century, the post–Vatican II period brought about several changes for the Church as a whole: a much weaker response of the laity toward the moral and doctrinal teaching of the pope and bishops; the deterioration of the link of obedience between bishops and lay movements; a growing pluralism within Catholicism and a culture of theological dissent from Church leadership; and the beginning of the detachment of the "civil society" in the Catholic Church— the laity—from Church institutions.[11] Italy and Italian Catholicism became the first and paradigmatic field of operation for these occurrences.[12]

CATHOLIC MOVEMENTS IN ITALY DURING AND AFTER 1968

From the historical point of view, the phenomenon of the new Catholic movements has much more to do with the "spirit" rather than the letter of the Council. As it has been observed recently, "One of the most striking developments in Catholic life since the Council ended has been the flourishing of 'movements' such as Opus Dei, the Neo-Catechumenate, Communion and Liberation, and so on."[13] This development happened also in Italy and greatly contributed to the changing landscape of Italian Catholicism and to the relationship between Italian political culture and the Italian church.

The issue of the role of Catholic movements in Italy after 1968 will be addressed by focusing on four different groups: Azione Cattolica (Catholic Action), Comunione e Liberazione (Communion and Liberation), Sant'Egidio, and the Organizations of Catholic Boy Scouts and Girl Scouts (ASCI, Associazione Scout Cattolici Italiani; AGI, Associazione Guide Italiane; later AGESCI, Associazione Guide e Scouts Cattolici Italiani). Omitted from this analysis are Catholic movements and organizations that did not confront the cultural and political situation around 1968, and whose cultural and political ties with Italy were much less important than their ties with other countries (that is, Spanish-speaking movements such as Opus Dei and the Legionaries of Christ on one hand, and charismatic-Pentecostal groups on the other).[14]

CATHOLIC ACTION: THE LAY ORGANIZATION PAR EXCELLENCE NO MORE

The oldest and noblest nest of Catholic laity was Catholic Action, founded in the 1920s by Pius XI in order to form and educate laymen and women in a society on the verge of being attacked or already under siege by Fascist, Nazi, and Communist ideologies.[15] Catholic Action was the organization par excellence of the Catholic laity in Italy, in connection with the Catholic Federation of University students (FUCI) and the organization of young Catholics (Gioventù Italiana di Azione Cattolica, GIAC), and acted as an umbrella organization for the Catholic laity in Italy. Diocese- and parish-based, Catholic Action enrolled its members through the territorial organization of the Church. Its first leaders were Giuseppe Lazzati, Carlo Carretto, Fr. Franco Costa, Fr. Emilio Guano, and Armida Barelli. In 1946, Vittorino

Veronese became president (with Luigi Gedda as vice president); Vittorio Bachelet was president for the crucial period 1964–73, with Fr. Franco Costa formally guaranteeing the obedience of the organization to the bishops and the pope as "ecclesiastical assistant" (1963–72). The intellectual sources of Catholic Action put this new kind of laity front and center in the attempt to renew the language of Catholic theology vis-à-vis the modern world. This is demonstrated by Jacques Maritain, the new ecclesiology overcoming the idea of the Church as a *societas perfecta* (a "perfect institution"), and in general, the cautious but at the same time attentive approach to the progressive *nouvelle théologie* that decisively influenced the theology of the Second Vatican Council.

Catholic Action, whose influence and power in the Catholic Church peaked in the late 1940s and 1950s, passed through Vatican II, gaining recognition in the Council documents as "the organization" par excellence of Catholic laity. Nevertheless, it was not able to take advantage of a "theology of the laity" that was canonically still incipient but culturally already exhausted, and in a sense pre–Vatican II. That is why Catholic Action started losing members in favor of the new movements immediately after Vatican II, just when it was accomplishing much more than the rest of the Catholic laity by accepting Vatican II, its ecclesiology of the Church as a communion, and the need to reconcile the Catholic laity with a more democratic organizational model.

In the post–Vatican II sixties in Italy, Catholic Action tried to walk the middle line, refusing the radical, anti-institutional mood also active among Catholics, and holding an open dialogue with the students' movement and society. But at the same time, Catholic Action embraced some cultural aspects of 1968: "Catholic Action lived the period of 1968 with attentiveness and openness of mind; in its younger components it created a profound relationship with that movement and through many of its members it became part of that movement of ideas that was 1968."[16]

The effort to stop the departure of its members with a new statute (October–November 1969) was only partially successful. The new statute disappointed both the liberal and the conservative wings of the movement because, on the one hand, it underscored the institutional continuity with the past, and on the other, it stressed the role of Catholic Action in promoting "the co-responsibility of laity in the mission of the Church."[17] But the new attention of Catholic Action for the political and social movements did not meet universal approval: "The new Statute had many supporters, but also caused dismay and disappointment, especially in the most extreme fringes of Catholic Action."[18]

The "religious option" (*scelta religiosa*, opposed to the partisan-political engagement of Catholic Action between World War II and Vatican II in Italy), the adoption of a framework typical of a democratic association (*scelta democratica* and *scelta associativa*), and the end of the political and institutional ties of Catholic Action members with the Christian-Democratic Party (Democrazia Cristiana) represented huge steps in the direction of a new, postconciliar identity of Catholic Action. But it was also an option that clearly went against the stream both of the 1968 movement and of the new Catholic movements: "The weaknesses of the post-Vatican II renewal of the Church were closely intertwined with the need for more genuineness, naturalness, and faithfulness to the Gospel, together with an anti-hierarchical and anti-institutional mood."[19]

The delay in updating its theological and political culture and the attempt to stand for the obedient, old guard of the Catholic laity cost Catholic Action many of its members after 1968. Apart from this political crisis of membership, the attempts of Catholic Action to reform itself in the early seventies were not rewarded by the Holy See, which soon started to repudiate its new, progressive theological course and sought new organizations of the new Italian laity that were more reliable than "the old guard" in the stormy period between 1968 and the seventies. The clash between Catholic Action and the Vatican, especially between 1970 and 1973, was caused by Catholic Action's new approach to the social and political realm, the so-called religious option, that was intended to give more autonomy to Italian lay Catholics about the legitimate pluralism of their political options and to distance itself from the influence of the Vatican and Italian bishops in Italian politics.[20]

During the 1980s and 1990s, the pontificate of John Paul II was much more explicit than Paul VI's in indicating the need for a new and stronger accountability of the Italian laity to the pope. This responsibility evidently was not to be found anymore in

Catholic Action, split "between conscience and obedience,"[21] that is, between fidelity to the Church and responsibility to the new and diverse cultural and political sensibility of its members. The late reconciliation between the Vatican and the Italian bishops, on one side, and Catholic Action, on the other, in Loreto in 2004, magnified not the rehabilitation of Catholic Action in the eyes of the Roman Church, but the new obedience of Catholic Action to the Holy See and the spectacular acknowledgment by Rome of the supremacy of the more assertive style of Communion and Liberation.[22]

COMMUNION AND LIBERATION: "WE ARE THE REAL SIXTIES"

Communion and Liberation, founded by Fr. Luigi Giussani in 1954 with the name of Gioventù Studentesca, represented the most significant Catholic movement in Milan and soon became the most important splinter group from Catholic Action in Italy. Luigi Giussani (1922–2005), the founder of the most politically active Catholic movement in Italy, had taught at the Seminary of Venegono near Milan, before teaching Catholic religion in a high school in Milan (1954–64) and holding the chair of introductory theology at the Catholic University of the Sacred Heart in Milan until 1990.[23] In 1965, Fr. Luigi Giussani left Gioventù Studentesca and founded the Charles Peguy Center in Milan—the beginning of the transition to what became the new movement, Communion and Liberation.[24] A charismatic leader of this new students' circle, Fr. Luigi Giussani had his disciples read Jacques Maritan, Charles Peguy, Paul Claudel, Georges Bernanos, but also American and Russian literature, and Jonathan Edwards. In the post–Vatican II period, this intellectual eclecticism eventually led Giussani to accept Henri de Lubac's emphasis on the issue of nature and grace in reaction against the anthropological theology of Karl Rahner and Edwaard Schillebeeckx.[25] Giussani's ecclesiology became increasingly autarchic, monolithic, and inclined to a quasi-identification of the Church with Christ. Communion and Liberation's understanding of Maritain is closer to his harsh judgment of Vatican II expressed in *Le paysan de la Garonne* (1967) than to the philosophy of *Humanisme integrale* (1936).[26] At the same time, the publishing house close to Communion and Liberation, Jaca Book, also published authors who were very popular among the revolt movement of 1968, such as Régis Debray, Fidel Castro, and Rosa Luxembourg.[27]

Evident far before the emergence of Communion and Liberation was Catholic Action's problematic involvement with the tumultuous Catholic 1960s in Italy, and the tensions within Catholic Action about the need for renewal and the legacy of the old heritage of an association founded in 1868.[28] According to Communion and Liberation, the events of 1968 played a major role because the students' movement attracted many members of the group led by Giussani, Gioventù Studentesca, causing the most serious crisis in the history of the group, which was reborn after 1968 and in opposition to the progressive culture of the 1960s. The historical account of the participation of Catholics in the 1968 movement by members of Communion and Liberation shows the heavy burden suffered by the group in those turbulent years.[29] The founder, Don Luigi Giussani, recalled these troubled times:

> The development of the movement became less clear in 1963–64, until the dark moment of 1968 that triggered the consequences of the previous 5–6 years, when the bad influence of a few people had radically changed the original idea and made the center of our action not our presence in the schools, but a vague social activism. Our identity was lost....The political project had taken the place of our presence, utopia had become the center. What happened between 1963 and 1968 was a process of adaptation and surrender to the environment.[30]

The harsh opposition to the students' protests in the late 1960s in Italy is clearly present in the ideological history of Giussani's group, notwithstanding the fact that many of its members had been part of that students' movement, as we can see in a speech that Fr. Giussani gave in 1976:

The historical trajectory had already made justice of *the vanity and emptiness of the utopia of 1968*: this utopia was nothing other than a tool for a *new hegemony, even more despotic and destructive*. That is why we continue to say that we are the only representatives of the real 1968.[31]

Communion and Liberation (CL) owes much of its good fortune and political success to 1968: while rejecting the evident Marxist ideological backdrop of the students' revolt, Communion and Liberation capitalized on the anti-institutional mood that became mainstream in the culture of CL. At the same time, CL contributed to the issue of the change in Church leadership by reacting against the post–Vatican II crisis of authority in the Church with a display of ultramontanist devotion for the pope.

The political language of Communion and Liberation, in the wake of the reconstruction of the group from scratch after the shock of 1968, changed its target but not its weapon. Simultaneously refusing the "people of God" ecclesiology of Vatican II and the liberal/progressive culture of the 1960s, in the early seventies, Communion and Liberation was the politically most engaged group in an Italian Catholicism that seemed paralyzed between the newly discovered Catholic "political theology" and the need to distance itself from the tradition of close collaboration of the Catholic Church in Italy with the Christian-Democratic Party (Democrazia Cristiana), the centrist party that ruled Italy for fifty years after the end of World War II:

> The Italian Catholic movement is embedded in a conciliar legacy that pushes it towards a more direct engagement with the world, but at the same time employing a cautious and realist strategy, which sometimes leads to some kind of desertion....Lay Catholics can escape this trap only by creating different and autonomous paths, thus initiating a diaspora that has not been studied yet.[32]

Despite the official and apologetically driven history of the movement, written by one of its most prominent members,[33] the ideological origins of Communion and Liberation shared the ideological attack against the liberal state with other Catholic movements and with the culture of the 1960s, as it has been acknowledged by its members: "*Gioventù Studentesca* expressed the same need for renewal as the students' movement did, but it judged the ways of the movement inadequate."[34] Communion and Liberation focused on the "culture of the presence" (that is, the visible presence in politics and in the economic system) of Catholics in society,[35] and rejected every political project and disqualifier of political engagement. According to Communion and Liberation, politics is radically disqualified as a field of action for Catholics: "Politics is just another trap created by the 'false rationality of the Enlightenment.'"[36]

While Italian Catholicism was struggling to get rid of the heavy burden of the clergy's political cooperation with the Christian-Democratic Party, Communion and Liberation pushed a small but important part of the Italian laity back into the "ghetto" under the flag of a renewed version of the early twentieth century *non expedit*: Italian Catholics can be politically active only under the umbrella of the Holy See. Communion and Liberation and its branches rejected the need for political mediation inside the Christian-Democratic Party, on one side, and bargained its social and economical resources with grassroots politicians from every political party, on the other, in order to fund branches of the group that specialized in providing welfare and social services (school, health care, jobs) for members of Communion and Liberation and their families.

Communion and Liberation took advantage of the last years of Paul VI's pontificate and comprehended before others the major shift in the pope's attitude toward Vatican II and the post-conciliar problems. The turning point in the success of Communion and Liberation came with John Paul II and his vision for new Catholicism in Italy. John Paul II's preference for the "new Catholic movements" and the antiliberal (even more than anti-Communist) language of Communion and Liberation developed very early in the history of his pontificate, and peaked in 1982 with the pope's visit to its annual meeting in Rimini.

The struggle against the anthropology of liberation of 1968 and John Paul II's emphasis on moral issues made Communion and Liberation a key player in the public arena of the Catholic

Church in Italy during the last pontificate of the twentieth century. In 1980, Fr. Giussani affirmed, "Communion and Liberation created a new synthesis, in a dialectic, practical, cultural, and educational opposition to 1968."[37]

The cultural opposition of Communion and Liberation against 1968 was also an opposition to the early attempt of Italian Catholicism and of some of the leaders of the Italian episcopate to accept democratic culture in order to finally savor the taste of the end of temporal power and new freedom for the Catholic Church at the end of the "Constantine era." Communion and Liberation's success in representing Italian Catholicism as "resilient" toward the novelty of Vatican II was rooted in the distance it took from the message of 1968. Nevertheless, the "Jacobin-minded" language of the new political elites of the 1960s still played a role in the propaganda of Communion and Liberation toward a renewal of the leading elites of the Church compromised with the social and political power of post-Catholic Italy.

Communion and Liberation rejected the 1960s because of the use of Marxist language and analysis in the movements, and because CL saw in the sixties an attack against the institutions of political, social, and religious power.[38] As its founder explained in a speech given in 1981, "Radicalism is just bourgeois ideology made into a penetrating and solid system. Bourgeois ideology is the extreme, final, and most coherent result of the anthropological and social views of the Enlightenment, of liberalism, and then also of Marxism."[39] But, at the same time, Communion and Liberation used social tactics similar to the leaders of the 1960s in order to affirm its presence and power in the heart of Italian Catholicism. The success of Giussani's group, which was unofficially recognized by Paul VI in 1975 and then greatly magnified by John Paul II, was paradigmatic of the crisis of the old Catholic elite (embodied by Catholic Action and especially by bishops whose relationships with Communion and Liberation were never unproblematic) and the success of the new Catholicism of the movements (strengthened by a direct papal endorsement of the movements' founders).

THE COMMUNITY OF SANT'EGIDIO: FOCUS ON THE POOR, PEACE, AND ECUMENISM

A particular community movement, distant from both the cradle of Catholic Action and from the other "new Catholic movements," was the 1968-born and Rome-based Comunità di Sant'Egidio. Founded by a young Italian layman, Andrea Riccardi, the Community of Sant'Egidio was one of the first expressions of the desire for an alternative to the institutional structures of the Catholic Church but remained detached from the ideological mood of 1968 and of the 1970s.[40] Born, like Communion and Liberation, from a group of students looking at a changing world as a field for personal engagement in society, Sant'Egidio developed a particular charisma that made it different not only from Communion and Liberation, but from every other "new Catholic movement."

Now one of the most important and widely published historians of the Catholic Church and the papacy,[41] Riccardi founded Sant'Egidio in 1968 with a group of high school students from the Liceo Virgilio in the bourgeois heart of Rome with the intent to remake the world in the image of the gospel, starting with charitable projects in the poor suburbs of Rome. Soon the community expanded beyond the boundaries of Rome, and its engagements became international when, in the 1990s, Sant'Egidio became active in the mediation between parties in several international conflicts.[42] This dimension was consistent with the later diplomatic engagements of the community, given that the city of Rome has been seen from antiquity as a shared place in a world burdened by nationalisms and ethnocentrisms.

This openness to the world—and not just "internationalization"—is the most typical sign of the specificity of Sant'Egidio in the landscape of the post–Vatican II Catholic movements. The typical marker of postconciliar Catholic movements—the core value of fidelity to the pope—was embodied in the Community of Sant'Egidio in two rather particular and uncommon elements in modern Italian Catholicism, very distant from Catholic Action as well as from Communion and Liberation. On one hand, the creation of an efficient and ecumenical welfare network in Rome for the poor, the homeless, and the immigrants—solidarity with the poor and solidarity with other cultures and societies[43]—was the Community of Sant'Egidio's translation of both Vatican II ecclesiology and 1968 political openness to the world, along with a political culture that did not reject liberal Catholicism but, on the contrary, accepted the end of confessionalism and thus the cultural basis of *Risorgimento* and the modern constitutional Italian Republic. On the other hand, the culture of the group (which at the beginning, did not share the typical 1968 passion for politics, assemblies, and democracy when it came to the life of their own movement) turned to a rather cultivated and antifundamentalist biblical culture, to the study of the history of ancient traditions of the undivided Christianity of the first millennium, and to ecumenism and interreligious dialogue. Riccardi repeated Sant'Egidio's particular relationship with 1968, defining himself "a child of 1968," that is, a citizen of the world and a member of the Church who learned that everything also has a political dimension.[44]

The event of the interreligious prayer for peace in Assisi (October 1986) marked the first international success of the movement, which soon became famous for its devotion to peacebuilding initiatives in Africa (especially Mozambique in 1992) and Eastern Europe (Albania, Kosovo in 1997–98), and the ongoing international campaign against the death penalty.

The success of the Community of Sant'Egidio in the following years represented the most remarkable example of the success of a postconciliar and post-1968 Catholic movement. Despite the "progressive" elements of its social activism and theological culture—which were quite unique for Italy—the fidelity to the pope as their bishop, but also as the Bishop of Rome, the head of the Catholic Church, protected this small but active group of young activists led by a group of intellectuals based in Rome, sometimes labeled "the United Nations of Trastevere": "The local Church of Rome and its bishop represent a very important reference point in such a big world."[45]

The balance embodied by the Community of Sant'Egidio between fidelity to the culture of Vatican II (the new role of the Bible, ecumenism, interreligious dialogue) and the traditional "Rome-centric Catholicism" (made up of an effective social network with members of the Roman Curia and of Roman politics) said a lot about the outcomes of the "Roman Catholic filtering of 1968": the activism of the laity and good relations with the Roman Curia; the skills in creating services of Catholic welfare together with effective cooperation with local governments (in the slums surrounding Rome as well as in HIV/AIDS-devastated Africa); the academic engagement in organizing international ecumenical and interreligious meetings along with deep cultural ties to Catholic tradition; and the caution and wariness for the political demands of the Catholic Church in Italy (concerning issues of Catholic schools, abortion, bioethics).

The importance of this lightly institutionalized movement lies more in its most visible national leaders than in the relatively small numbers of members scattered in some cities in Italy and around the world. The informal and personal ties with the leadership of the leftist Democratic Party and the change of pontificate with Benedict XVI did not seem to endanger the role of the Community of Sant'Egidio on the stage of Italian Catholicism.

CATHOLIC BOY SCOUTS AND GIRL SCOUTS ASSOCIATIONS: FROM PARAMILITARY CULTURE TO ANTIAUTHORITARIANISM

On the left side of Italian Catholicism, the associations of Catholic Boy Scouts (Associazione Scout Cattolici Italiani, ASCI) and Catholic Girl Scouts (Associazione Guide Italiane, AGI) represented the most receptive part of Catholic laity both to the message of Vatican II and to the culture of the 1960s.[46] Created in Italy only a few years after its beginnings in England, thanks to Italian nobles close to the English-expatriate community living in Italy, after World War II the comeback of the Catholic Scout movement in Italy (which Mussolini had outlawed in 1928 in order to gain complete control over the education of the younger generations of the Fascist state) followed the guidelines of the faithfulness of Catholic organizations to the Church of Pius XII and shaped itself along the cultural and spiritual identity of the "Franco-Belgian school" of scouting. Close to the theological identity of the Jounesse Ouvrière Chrétienne and, more generally, to Catholic Action in Europe before and after World War II, the Italian Catholic Scout movement advocated a special educational methodology but did not, until the 1970s, express the desire to part ways with the mainstream Catholic lay movements in Italy.[47] After Vatican II, the Italian Catholic Scout movement represented an important part of the Italian laity because of their numbers (eighty-three thousand in 1974, almost two hundred thousand in the late 1990s). Both the male and female Italian Catholic Scout organizations—which have a difficult relationship with the bishops and pope due to the Catholic Scouts' inferiority complex relative to Catholic Action—successively merged in 1974 to form the new association, AGESCI (Associazione Guide e Scout Cattolici Italiani).

The sensitivity to the importance of some of the theological as well as cultural and pedagogical issues of the 1960s for the Catholic Scout movement were common to both the Boy and Girl Scouts association and to their leadership: the new role of the laity in the Church conceived as the "people of God"; the need for a gradual "demilitarization" of traditional Boy Scout language (founded in 1907 by an English lieutenant general, Robert Baden-Powell); the option for coeducation (boys and girls educated together by a mixed staff of educators and a parish priest); the option to establish an association based on a "pledge" (engagement in the sociopolitical reality, in the sense of Fr. Lorenzo Milani's *I care*), functioning with democratic rules, resenting the traditional Catholic anticommunism and accepting antifascism as a common ground, as proclaimed in the Patto Associativo (the "mission statement" of the AGESCI) in 1974; the assumption of a pedagogical methodology following antiauthoritarianism more from Maria Montessori than from the anti-institutionalism of 1968; and disengagement from any direct involvement of the association with party politics.

On the other side, the Catholic Scout movement in Italy was important because it featured one of the most successful experiences in reconciling the culture of 1968 and Catholicism. This was despite some of its clearly opposing elements: the option not to follow the 1968 anti-institutional mood concerning the strong role of the educator in the education process; the intact role of "outside life," while urban sociology played a major role in shaping the ideological landscape of 1968; an expressed intention to remain faithful to the Catholic Church (following the example of Fr. Milani) while playing a vanguard role in some typical tenets of the Catholic Church's idea of education (male and female coeducation, lay ministry in the Church, a secondary role for the clergy in the life of the local Scout groups).

It is noteworthy that AGI (the Girl Scouts association) pushed much harder than ASCI (the Boy Scouts association) in accepting the new ideas of the 1960s and in shaping the merger of the two associations, which was recognized—not without difficulties—by the Catholic Church only years later. But for the Catholic Scout movement in Italy, the impact with 1968 went in multiple directions. First, the antiauthoritarian culture of the 1960s posed a cultural challenge to the educational method of *Scouting for Boys*, conceived of at the beginning of the twentieth century by Robert Baden-Powell after the Second Boer War in South Africa. Second, the merger typical of 1968 between the private and public dimensions of individual life provided the educational intuition of the boy scout methodology about moral self-improvement and sociopolitical dimension with issues regarding the "elitism" of the educational model of scouting. Third, and most important, 1968 redefined the relationship between membership in a Catholic association and faithfulness to every aspect of the Catholic magisterium.[48]

Not by accident, between 1974 and 1975, there was a long exchange of pointed discussions between the leaders of the Italian Catholic Scout movement and the Italian Bishops' Conference, especially concerning the faithfulness of the new association AGESCI to the Catholic Church and the need to avoid a direct politicization of the activities of the association. In particular, the Scout association reassured the bishops by stating the goals of the movement: "To make the educational activities of the association engaged in the big social problems close to the members' lives, even the ones that are not visible....We want to offer our educational activities also to the most poor and marginalized boys and girls."[49]

But the crisis in the relationship with the Italian bishops was soon resolved and the new association AGESCI saw a steady rise in the number of its members through the 1970s and 1980s, until the 1990s when it reached two hundred thousand members in

Italy. By then it was known as a unique Catholic organization that had gained the respect of society and of the Church despite an unparalleled independence from the Roman Catholic hierarchy and a variegated spectrum of political ideologies among its members and leaders.[50]

The national events held by AGESCI for its educators in 1986 and 1997 marked the distinctiveness of the Catholic Scout association in Italy. It specialized in the education of the younger generation with a classical but updated methodology, distant from any direct involvement in national politics. Even though the cultural and theological roots of Fr. Lorenzo Milani (1923–67) and Fr. Giuseppe Dossetti (1913–96) are undeniably much more "traditional" (without being traditionalist) and "conservative" (without being aligned with right-wing political parties) than their political reception by the progressives in Italian Catholicism of the 1970s, the cultural ties of the Italian Scout movement with the progressive, socially and politically engaged Catholicism embodied by the followers of Fr. Milani and Fr. Dossetti are very evident.[51] The remarkable "naiveté" of the leadership of AGESCI concerning their relationship with the Catholic Church, which continues to look at the largest and most active Catholic association in Italy as the most independent and self-governing player in the field of Italian laity, explains the recent comeback of the most traditionalist part of Catholic scouting (Scoutes d'Europe) at the court of Benedict XVI's Roman Curia.[52]

CONCLUSIONS: THE NEW CATHOLIC MOVEMENTS AND THE NEW CATHOLIC ELITE IN ITALY

The difficulties in the transformation of Italian Catholicism from the pre–Vatican II model are often portrayed as a direct result of Vatican II Catholics' embracing of the radical left-wing political culture of 1968. This brief synthesis of the encounter between the 1960s and Italian Catholic lay movements offers a different picture: much of the post–Vatican II Catholicism in Italy was shaped by the new Catholic movements and their interpretation of 1968. This change called "1968" was actually part of the backdrop of the "new Catholic movements"—as well as of the movements, such as Communion and Liberation, that Catholic apologists now frequently identify as the Church's best possible defense against the surrender to secularization brought about by 1968.

There was an intertwining of the reception of Vatican II with Catholics' participation in 1968, and Italian Catholicism made a real contribution to the tumultuous 1960s and 1970s. The different identities of the Italian church survived as long as they managed to establish a link with the bishops and the National Bishops' Conference, Conferenza Episcopale Italiana, and its pastoral projects launched in the 1970s: the radical culture of Communion and Liberation and the edgy pastoral outreach of Italian Catholic Scouting became safe because they were under the aegis of the Italian bishops.[53] Sant'Egidio found a powerful sponsor in the Bishop of Rome. In this respect, it is clear that the ideological DNA of the new Catholic movements and their relationship with 1968 soon became secondary.

The most important outcomes of the link between Vatican II and 1968 are not just in terms of the theological and cultural change of paradigm, but also in terms of the change in the elites of Italian Catholicism. The final outcome of the Council's reception in Italy was very distant from the much-imagined and dreamed-of Church led by the bishops of Vatican II, but no less distant from the idea of an Italian Catholicism as victim of the dialogue between theologians of Vatican II and liberal and Marxist groups. Even a political scientist such as Nicola Matteucci observed in 1970 that in Italian Catholicism, two types of cultures were active: the "Catholic culture," made up of different cultural origins and markers, and the "Catholic ghetto," the great organizations built by the Catholic Church in opposition to "modern civilization." According to Matteucci, the new Catholic movements born after 1968 did not represent the ultimate surrender to theological liberalism, but they were the successors of the same old antimodern soul of the Catholic ghetto: the same intolerant culture at the service of a new, self-serving view of modernity.[54] There is some truth in the opinion of an admirer of American political culture, such as Nicola Matteucci, about the relationship between 1968 and the new Catholic movements. Among the issues of the new Catholic movements close to the culture of 1968, there was the emancipation of the laity from the clergy through the delegitimization of theology, the creation of a new, deinstitutionalized model of Church, and a more pluralistic and more engaged relationship with politics.[55] All of this was expressed in a language rife with egalitarianism, Jacobinism, and harsh criticism of the modern state.[56]

Thus it is not surprising the fact that moderate reformist Catholics (mostly in Catholic Action) became more and more marginal in Italy during the Catholic 1960s and 1970s. The Catholic scout association AGESCI preserved its independence and courage in experimenting with new pedagogical and social instruments, but it never had nor desired to "have a seat at the table" of decision making in the post–Vatican II Catholic Church.[57] The real winners of the struggle within Italian Catholicism after 1968 were movements like Communion and Liberation on one side, and the Community of Sant'Egidio on the other, which embodied and represented the Rome-linked and at the same time postinstitutional face of Roman Catholicism—while expressing two very different sets of styles and theological cultures.

The overall result of the rise of the Catholic movements in the last forty years—with their dramatic breakups and divisions between the radicals on one side and the ecclesiastical institution on the other—was not just the newly begun Church reform sparked by the spirit of Vatican II but also the pluralist face of Italian Catholicism made up of Catholic movements, all of them having dealt with every part of the diverse culture of 1968 and of the politically dangerous 1970s, absorbing some parts and rejecting others.

The result of the movements' desire to distance themselves from the radicalism of 1968 (the dissent) as well as from the reformism of the realist interpreters of Vatican II (the laity of Catholic Action, the bishops) was the creation of a new elite inside the movements, the *homines novi*. This phenomenon of the new Catholic movement has already gone beyond the geographical boundaries of Italy: understanding their cultural roots—one of them being 1968—is the key to understanding their historical importance in twentieth-century Catholicism.

Notes

1. See Hans Küng, *La Chiesa* (Brescia: Queriniana, 1969); *The Church*, trans. Ray Ockenden and Rosaleen Ockenden (New York: Sheed and Ward, 1967); original German *Die Kirche* (Freiburg i.B.: Herder, 1967).

2. See *Il dossier del Catechismo olandese*, ed. Leo Alting von Geusau and Fernando Vittorino Joannes (Milan: Mondadori, 1968); *A New Catechism: Catholic Faith for Adults*, trans. from the Dutch by Kevin Smyth (New York: Herder and Herder, 1967).

3. See Alberto Melloni, "Movimenti. De significatione verborum," *I movimenti nella Chiesa*, ed. Alberto Melloni, special issue of *Concilium* 3 (2003): 13–35.

4. John W. O'Malley, *What Happened at Vatican II* (Cambridge, MA: Belknap Press of Harvard University Press, 2008), 53–92.

5. See Giuseppe Alberigo, "Il concilio Vaticano II e le trasformazioni culturali in Europa," *Cristianesimo nella Storia*, 20, no. 2 (1999): 383–405; *History of Vatican II*, ed. Giuseppe Alberigo, vols. 1–5 (Leuven-Bologna: Peeters-Il Mulino, 1995–2001); English version ed. Joseph A. Komonchak (Maryknoll, NY: Orbis, 1995–2006).

6. See Richard P. McBrien, *The Church: The Evolution of Catholicism* (New York: Harper, 2008), 345–49; Richard R. Gaillardetz, *Ecclesiology for a Global Church: A People Called and Sent* (Maryknoll, NY: Orbis, 2008), 132–42.

7. See Giuseppe Alberigo, "Santa Sede e vescovi nello Stato unitario. Verso un episcopato italiano (1958–1985)," in *La Chiesa e il potere politico* (Turin: Einaudi, 1986), 857–79; Alberto Melloni, "Da Giovanni XXIII alle Chiese italiane del Vaticano II," in *Storia dell'Italia religiosa. 3. L'età contemporanea*, ed. Gabriele De Rosa, Tullio Gregory, and André Vauchez (Rome-Bari: Laterza, 1995), 361–403; Guido Verucci, "La chiesa postconciliare," in *Storia dell'Italia repubblicana* (Turin: Einaudi, 1995), 297–382; Augusto D'Angelo, "L'episcopato italiano dalla frammentazione al profilo nazionale," *Memoria e ricerca* 12 (2003): 75–92.

8. On "leftist Catholicism," see Gerd-Rainer Horn, *The Spirit of '68: Rebellion in Western Europe and North America, 1956–1976* (New York: Oxford University Press, 2007).

9. "Non si può dire che la componente religiosa abbia giocato un ruolo decisivo": Agostino Giovagnoli, "Cattolici nel Sessantotto," *1968 tra utopia e Vangelo. Contestazione e mondo cattolico*, ed. Agostino Giovagnoli (Rome: AVE, 2000), 39.

10. "Cette presence des catholiques au sein du mouvement de contestation fut moins marginale qu'on pourrait le supposer": Salvatore

Abbruzzese, *Comunione e Liberazione, Identité Catholique et Disqualifica-tion du monde* (Paris: Cerf, 1989), 117.

11. See Carlo Falconi, *La contestazione nella Chiesa. Storia e docu-menti del movimento cattolico antiautoritario in Italia e nel mondo* (Milan: Feltrinelli, 1969); Igino Giordani, *La Chiesa della contestazione* (Rome: Città Nuova, 1970); Danièle Hervieu-Léger, *De la mission à la protesta-tion. L'évolution des étudiants chrétiens en France (1965–1970)* (Paris: Cerf, 1973).

12. On the 1970s in Italy, see Guido Crainz, *Il paese mancato: dal miracolo economico agli anni Ottanta* (Rome: Donzelli, 2003); Alberto Melloni, "L'occasione mancata. Appunti sulla chiesa italiana, 1978–2009," in *Il Vangelo basta*, ed. Alberto Melloni (Rome: Carocci, 2010).

13. Nicholas Lash, *Theology for Pilgrims* (Notre Dame, IN: Univer-sity of Notre Dame Press, 2008), 236.

14. For a general overview on the postconciliar Catholic move-ments, see Agostino Favale, *Movimenti ecclesiali contemporanei. Dimen-sioni storiche, teologico-spirituali ed apostoliche* (Rome: LAS, 1991).

15. See Liliana Ferrari, *L'Azione cattolica in Italia dalle origini al pon-tificato di Paolo VI* (Brescia: Queriniana, 1982); Liliana Ferrari, *Una storia dell'Azione cattolica: gli ordinamenti statutari da Pio XI a Pio XII* (Genoa: Marietti, 1989).

16. "L'Azione Cattolica visse con attenzione e spirito di apertura la stagione del Sessantotto; mediante le sue componenti giovanili stabilì un contatto profondo e attraverso numerose persone si può dire che fece parte di quel movimento di idee": Angelo Bertani, "L'Azione Cattolica Italiana e la svolta del Concilio," in *1968 tra utopia e Vangelo*, 79–101, quotation on 79–80.

17. Ernesto Preziosi, *Obbedienti in piedi. La vicenda dell'Azione Cattolica in Italia* (Turin: SEI, 1996), 318–25.

18. "Il nuovo Statuto suscitò molti consensi, ma anche sconcerto e scontento, soprattutto nelle ali più estreme dell'ACI": Mario Casella, *L'Azione Cattolica nell'Italia contemporanea (1919–1969)* (Rome: AVE, 1992), 555.

19. "Esigenze di genuinità, di spontaneità, di rigore evangelico, raf-forzate dalla ventata antigerarchica e anti-istituzionale, si intrecciarono strettamente alle debolezze presenti nel rinnovamento conciliare della chiesa italiana. Rispetto alla contestazione verso la gerarchia e la politi-cizzazione la scelta religiosa andava palesemente controcorrente": Guido Formigoni, *L'Azione Cattolica Italiana* (Milan: Ancora, 1988), 111.

20. See Azione Cattolica Italiana, *Scelta religiosa e politica: docu-menti 1969–1988*, ed. Raffaele Cananzi (Rome: AVE, 1988); Mario

Casella, *Il magistero dei papi sull'Azione Cattolica. Da Pio IX a Francesco (1868–2013)* (Rome: AVE, 2014).

21. Vittorio De Marco, *Storia dell'Azione Cattolica negli anni Settanta* (Rome: Città Nuova, 2007).

22. See Alberto Melloni, "The Politics of the 'Church' in the Italy of Pope Wojtyła," *Journal of Modern Italian Studies* 12, no. 1 (2007): 60–85.

23. The first writings of Luigi Giussani—*Riflessioni sopra un'esperienza* (1959), *Tracce d'esperienza cristiana* (1960), and *Appunti di metodo cristiano* (1964)—had been published "pro manuscript," and they had been republished with the title *Tracce d'esperienza cristiana* (Milan: Jaca Book, 1972). For recent, sympathetic studies on Fr. Giussani, see Alberto Savorana, *Vita di don Giussani* (Milan: Rizzoli, 2013); Massimo Camisasca, *Don Giussani. La sua esperienza dell'uomo e di Dio* (Milan: San Paolo, 2009); Francesco Ventorino, *Luigi Giussani. La sfida della modernità* (Turin: Lindau, 2014).

24. Abbruzzese, *Comunione e Liberazione*, 105.

25. See Dadder, *Comunione e Liberazione. Phänomenologie einer neuen geistlichen Bewegung* (Konstanz: UVK, 2002), 154–71.

26. See ibid., 247–65. See Jacques Maritain, *Le paysan de la Garonne: Une vieux laïc s'interroge à propos du temps présent* (Paris: Desclèe De Brouwer, 1966). Translated by Michael Cuddihy and Elizabeth Hughes as *The Peasant of the Garonne: An Old Layman Questions Himself about the Present Time* (New York: Holt, Rinehart and Winston, 1968).

27. See Abbruzzese, *Comunione e Liberazione*, 107. On the relationship between social engagement of Catholics and domestic terrorism in Italy in the 1970s, see Guido Panvini, *Cattolici e violenza politica. L'altro album di famiglia del terrorismo italiano* (Padua: Marsilio, 2014).

28. On Communion and Liberation, see also *Gli estremisti di centro: il neo-integralismo cattolico degli anni '70. Comunione e liberazione. Presentazione di David Maria Turoldo*, ed. Sandro Bianchi and Angelo Turchini (Rimini-Florence: Guaraldi, 1975); Massimo Camisasca, *Comunione e Liberazione. Le origini (1954–1968)* (Cinisello Balsamo: San Paolo, 2001); Massimo Camisasca, *Comunione e Liberazione. La ripresa (1969–1976)*, (Cinisello Balsamo: San Paolo, 2003); Massimo Camisasca, *Comunione e Liberazione. Il riconoscimento (1976–1984). Appendice 1985–2005* (Cinisello Balsamo: San Paolo, 2006).

29. See Roberto Beretta, *Il lungo autunno. Controstoria del Sessantotto cattolico* (Milan: Rizzoli, 1998); Beretta, *Cantavamo Dio è morto. Il '68 dei cattolici* (Casale Monferrato: Piemme, 2008).

30. "La storia del movimento incominciò ad annebbiarsi nel '63–'64, fino alle tenebre del '68 che fece esplodere le conseguenze di quei cinque o sei anni in cui l'influsso di certe persone aveva capovolto la situazione

originale e reso scopo del nostro muoverci non la presenza nella scuola, ma un progetto d'attività sociale. Così l'identità stessa della nostra presenza si smarrì....Il progetto aveva sostituito la presenza, l'utopia l'aveva scalzata. Ciò che avvenne dal '63–'64 fino allo scoppio del '68 fu un processo di adattamento e di cedimento all'ambiente." Luigi Giussani, "Dall'utopia alla presenza" (1976), in Luigi Giussani, *Dall'utopia alla presenza (1975–1978)*, with a preface by Julián Carrón (Milan: Rizzoli, 2006), 63–64.

31. "La traiettoria storica aveva già sgomberato *la vanità e la vuotezza delle utopie del '68*: quello che esse avevano destato non era diventato altro che strumento *per una nuova egemonia, ancora più dispotica e livellatrice*. Perciò, già due-tre anni fa dicevamo di essere rimasti gli unici a portare avanti le parole del '68": ibid., 64–65.

32. "Le mouvement catholique italien se trouve ainsi coincé dans un héritage conciliaire qui le pousse aux engagements dans le monde et une stratégie réaliste de 'désertion' et de prudence. Les militants catholiques ne pourront sortir de ce piège qu'en prenant des chemins autonome set diversifiés, constituant ainsi une diaspora dont l'analyse est encore loin d'être fait." Salvatore Abbruzzese, *Comunione e Liberazione*, 127.

33. See Massimo Camisasca, *Comunione e Liberazione*, vol. 2: *La ripresa, 1969–1976* (Cinisello Balsamo: San Paolo, 2003).

34. "*Gioventù Studentesca* condivise l'istanza di rinnovamento insita nel Movimento studentesco, ma giudicò inadeguata la forma di lotta scelta": Maurizio Vitali and Ambrogio Pisoni, *Comunione e Liberazione* (Milan: Ancora, 1988), 77.

35. See Italo Mancini, *Tornino i volti* (Genoa: Marietti, 1988).

36. "Le politique n'est qu'un des pièges de la 'fausse rationalité des Lumières,'" in Abbruzzese, *Comunione e Liberazione*, 134.

37. "Comunione e Liberazione è sorta proprio come una nuova sintesi, in dialettica, in opposizione culturale e pratica, culturale ed educativa con il Sessantotto." Camisasca, *Comunione e Liberazione*, 56.

38. Ibid., 61–62.

39. "Il radicalismo non è nient'altro che il borghesismo eretto a sistema nel modo più coerente e capillare. Il borghesismo è l'esito estremo, ultimo e più coerente, di tutta quanta l'impostazione antropologica e sociale dell'Illuminismo, del liberalismo e quindi anche del marxismo." Luigi Giussani, "Qualcosa che cambia la vita" (1981), in Giussani, *Certi di alcune grandi cose (1979–1981)* (Milan: Rizzoli, 2007), 427.

40. See Hanspeter Oschwald, *Bibel, Mystik und Politik. Die Gemeinschaft Sant'Egidio* (Freiburg i.B.: Herder, 1996).

41. Among Andrea Riccardi's vast bibliography: *Il Partito romano nel secondo dopoguerra, 1945–1954* (Brescia: Queriniana, 1983); *Il potere del papa: da Pio XII a Paolo VI* (Rome-Bari: Laterza, 1988); *Il Vaticano e*

Mosca 1940–1990 (Rome-Bari: Laterza, 1992); *L'inverno più lungo 1943-44: Pio XII, gli ebrei e i nazisti a Roma* (Rome-Bari: Laterza, 2008).

42. See Andrea Riccardi, *Sant'Egidio, Rome et le monde. Entretiens avec Jean-Dominique Durand et Régis Ladous* (Paris: Ladous, 1996), 17 and 20.

43. See ibid., 27 and 110.

44. Ibid., 32.

45. "L'église de Rome et son évêque représentent un point de reference important dans un monde si grand, mais où resurgissent les frontiers." Ibid., 161.

46. See Mario Sica, *Storia dello scautismo in Italia*, 4th ed. (Rome: Fiordaliso, 1973, 2006).

47. See *Le scoutisme. Quel type d'hommes et quel type de femmes? Quel type de chrétiens?*, ed. Gérard Cholvy and Marie-Thérèse Cheroutre (Paris: Cerf, 1994).

48. A long, interesting series of interviews with members and leaders of the Catholic Scout movement in Italy between 1967 and the early seventies is in Vincenzo Schirripa, *Giovani sulla frontiera. Guide e Scout cattolici nell'Italia repubblicana (1943–1974)* (Rome: Studium, 2006), esp. 183–220.

49. "Il Consiglio Generale AGESCI ribadisce quindi la volontà associativa di essere lontani da ogni settarismo, e l'impegno a lottare contro ogni violenza, comunque e dovunque avvenga, e ad offrire la possibilità di una educazione e di una presenza scout anche negli ambienti più poveri ed emarginati," the response of the members of the Consiglio Generale of AGESCI to the Permanent Board of the Conferenza Episcopale Italiana, April 27, 1975, sent after the letter of the secretary of the Conferenza Episcopale Italiana, Enrico Bartoletti, April 24, 1975 to the Consiglio Generale of AGESCI, in *Documenti pontifici sullo Scautismo*, eds. Giovanni Morello and Francesco Pieri (Milan: Ancora, 1991), 242–45, quotation on 245.

50. See Achille Ardigò, Costantino Cipolla, and Stefano Martelli, *Scouts oggi: diecimila rovers/scolte dell'Agesci rispondono* (Rome: Borla, 1989).

51. See Laura Giuliani, *I giovani cattolici e la politica. Un'indagine su due realtà associative: AGESCI e RnS* (Milan: Angeli, 2003).

52. On the conservative branch of the European Catholic Scout movement, see *Leggere le tracce. Guide e scouts d'Europa nella Fraternità internazionale* (Rome: Paoline, 2007).

53. Vittorio De Marco, *Storia dell'Azione Cattolica negli anni Settanta* (Rome: Città Nuova, 2007), 242.

54. Nicola Matteucci, "La cultura politica italiana: fra l'insorgenza

populistica e l'età delle riforme," *Il Mulino* 19 (1970): 5–23, also in *Sul Sessantotto. Crisi del riformismo e "insorgenza populistica" nell'Italia degli anni Sessanta*, ed. Roberto Pertici (Soveria Mannelli: Rubbettino, 2008).

55. See Sandro Magister, *La politica vaticana e l'Italia 1943–1978* (Rome: Editori Riuniti, 1979).

56. See Guido Verucci, "Il 1968, il mondo cattolico italiano e la Chiesa," *Passato e presente* 20–21 (Dec. 1989): 107–22.

57. See Massimo Faggioli, "Tra chiesa territoriale e chiese personali. I movimenti ecclesiali nel post-concilio Vaticano II," in *I movimenti nella storia del cristianesimo. Caratteristiche—variazioni—continuità* ed. Giuseppe Alberigo and Massimo Faggioli, *Cristianesimo nella Storia* 24, no. 3 (2003): 677–704.

International Catholic Movements in the Postconciliar Period

The Implementation of Vatican II in Italy

INTRODUCTION

THE CENTRAL ROLE of the new Catholic movements is certainly one of the characteristics of postconciliar Catholicism, its theology, ecclesiology, spirituality, and its institutional model. Their range consists of Communion and Liberation, the Community of Sant'Egidio, the Focolare, the Neocatechumenal Way, Charismatic Catholics, and the Cursillo movement and is made up of groups, associations, and networks that are phenomenologically linked by the definition of *movement*, and should be studied in relation to Vatican II—to which they refer, although often more in search of legitimacy rather than in historical-theological terms. In this sense, the new Catholic movements represent a phenomenon typical of the postconciliar Church: they are an embodiment of the spirit of Vatican II but, at the same time, a challenge to a comprehensive historical understanding of the Council.

It is impossible to undertake a study of how Vatican II was implemented without an analysis of the growth of these groups that is independent of the self-definitions and self-representations that these movements—like any other human community—build around their own identity.[1] To limit this study to a celebration of these movements as the "fruit of Vatican II" would greatly simplify the richness of the conciliar corpus, but would also distort the hitherto underestimated (or sometimes denigrated) work of implementation carried out by movements in relation to the Council.[2] The issue, in fact, revolves not around the existence of a link between the Second Vatican Council and the phenomenon of the new Catholic movements—a link that is difficult to either deny or affirm outright[3]—but plays on the relationship between these two central points in the development of contemporary Catholicism and, on a theological and phenomenal level, the undeniable discontinuity between the preconciliar and conciliar periods,[4] and between the conciliar and the postconciliar periods, as the Church became aware of the "secular age."[5]

It is useful to remember that during the pontificates of Pius XI and Pius XII, all "Catholic movements" were included—especially in Europe—under the umbrella of Catholic Action, which was conceived not as a "movement" but as an extension of the Church hierarchy and part of the institutional Church. Catholic Action was closely focused on the authority of the pope, rather than around the bishops or the ailing political aspects of Catholicism, and it remained the main organization for the Catholic laity for a long time, at least four decades. Even during Vatican II, the issue about these types of movements, in the plural, found no forum in Council deliberations or in the conciliar commissions. This was, in part, due to the classic setting of the debate on the lay apostolate, even within a new assessment of the laity by conciliar ecclesiology; but it was also partly due to the postponement of the organizational and canonical issues in the postconciliar reform of the Code of Canon Law.[6] But the scenario, outside the Council, was already in the process of change. The shift in European Catholicism from a purely institutional Church to a Church more and more made of movements were part of an expression of a change that manifested itself in different ways in other regions of global Catholicism.[7]

Between the beginning of the sixties and the end of Paul VI's pontificate (1963–78), the rise of ecclesial movements took on the characteristics of a slow progression of phenomena that were individual and independent of each other but were all linked to a cultural, social, and political climate, rather than to a theological school or devotional style. Each followed its own different trajectory: dependent not only on the charisma of the founder and their underlying theological choices, but also on the conditions of their original local churches—their theological and spiritual tradition, the political and social scenario, and the characteristics of their held beliefs. The movements that survived that impetuous phase of founding new communities and associations, in their search for new forms of faith life, had to quickly deal with the difficulty of obtaining from the ecclesiastical establishment—from the bishops and then from Rome—recognition of a new formula for faith communities, which was *extra legem* regarding their canonical status.[8] In this sense, the trajectory of the new Catholic movements shows some similarities with the history of the relationship between the Vatican and American Catholicism between the nineteenth century and the late twentieth century: from a totally new institutional model seen with mistrust by the institutional Church, to a period of cautious acceptance, to a stage when the new model is presented as "the model" for the whole global Church.

The transition between Vatican II and the post-Council periods coincided with the stabilization and institutionalization of some elements that had come into being many years before, through a long and uneven evolution.[9] All the movements followed different routes that were more or less dramatic, more or less rooted in contemporary Catholicism, often pursuing a strategy of spreading internationally that showed the vitality and plurality of Catholicism, which, even if it was not always "extrainstitutional," in many cases, was avowedly "nonepiscopal" or "bishop-less," and closer to the style of a "community of life" than to the traditional Catholic ecclesiology of a local church led by its bishop.[10]

Later, we will give a comparison of the role of the movements that have a stronger Italian identity (such as Communion and Liberation and the Community of Sant'Egidio) and those that have a distinctive canonical identity that is in some sense "marginal" compared to the phenomenon of the movements (such as Opus Dei and the Regnum Christi of the Legionaries of Christ). However, here we will attempt to outline some lines of development that are common and distinct among some Catholic movements that have an international presence (Focolare, the Neocatechumenal Way, Charismatic Renewal, Catholic Scouts) and make some assumptions about their contribution to how Vatican II was implemented in Italy,[11] not because Italy is the model for the development of the new Catholic movements, but because Italy—for its geo-historical centrality for Catholic history—plays a particular role in the development of these new entities also in other cultural contexts. Tracing the first steps in Italy of new international Catholic movements is essential to understand their theological and ecclesiological itinerary.

THE FOCOLARE

Long before the founding of new movements took on the form and size of a wide-ranging diaspora in the history of the Catholic laity, during the postwar period, some autonomous groups coming out of Catholic Action had already taken shape in Italy. These were destined to become more original and eloquent than any of the other contemporary Catholic movements.[12] In 1947, the Opera di Maria (Work of Mary, which became Focolare) obtained the approval of the diocesan bishop of Trent. The group was founded by Chiara Lubich, an elementary school teacher who grew up in Catholic circles of Trent, where she was part of Catholic Action and the Franciscan Third Order. In 1948, the first male Focolare center was opened in Trent. In Rome, Chiara Lubich met the politician Igino Giordani, and he became the first married *focolarino*. In 1954, a branch for diocesan priests and religious members of the movement was founded, and in 1956, the first issue of *Città Nuova* was published.[13]

In 1962, John XXIII approved the Opera di Maria *ad experimentum*, which in the summer of 1959, had gathered together in the Trent region, in Northern Italy, more than ten thousand people from twenty-seven different countries; the first Mariapolis center for the training of members of the movement was founded in 1963 in Rocca di Papa, near Rome. In October 1965, Paul VI approved the Statute of the General Council of the Focolare, a movement that embraced *Ad Gentes* (the Second Vatican Council's Decree on the Missionary Activity of the Church) and the affirmation that the Spirit "through the seed of the Word and the preaching of the Gospel calls all people to Christ."[14] 1966 saw the creation of the youth arm of Opera di Maria. That same year, Chiara Lubich was received by the archbishop of Canterbury, Michael Ramsey, who encouraged her to spread the spirituality of the Focolare Movement in the Anglican Church in England; in 1967, it was the turn of Athenagoras, the Ecumenical Patriarch of Constantinople.

The founders of the movement in Italy, beginning in Trent, soon addressed themselves to Rome, with a trajectory that is common to all Catholic movements of twentieth century (and even to religious orders since the tenth century), in order to find acceptance and recognition by the pope. In 1948, the Focolare headquarters moved to Rome, while from 1949 to 1959, Mariapolis summer retreats were held at Fiera di Primiero and in Val di Fassa in the mountain region in Northern Italy near Trento. In 1950, there was a Focolare branch in Milan, and in 1953, one in Parma, but in 1960, a Mariapolis took place in Fribourg in Switzerland, and the worldwide dimension of the movement soon became decisive, with the creation of the first three international centers in Loppiano, Cameroon, and Argentina.[15] In 1952, the movement already made itself present in Europe; in 1958, in the United States; in 1963, in Africa; and from 1966 to 1967, in Asia and Oceania.

In the case of the Focolare, shifting their focus to Rome seems to have been intended to create a true center of unity around a single Focolare center, rather than a strategic move (as in the case of other movements) meant to employ the Roman headquarters only as the "diplomatic representation" of the movement at the Holy See. The international center of Rocca di Papa and the early and rapid creation of Mariapolis retreats worldwide bear witness to the international spreading of the movement on the one hand. But on the other hand, the proliferation of many centers of the movement are also indicative of the final transfer of the original core of the Focolare from Northern Italy to a less Italian base, one less characterized by a Catholic tradition and culture that were national or regional, in favor of a radically international dimension that was much more responsive to the ecumenical vocation of the movement.[16] Nevertheless, after the death of Chiara Lubich, the election of Maria Voce as president of the Focolare in July 2008 showed the importance of an Italian (and female) line of succession to lead the movement.

THE NEOCATECHUMENAL WAY

It was not just Italy that gave birth to the new lay groups. After Opus Dei and the Cursillo, in 1964, Spain witnessed the founding, in a shantytown on the outskirts of Madrid, of the Neocatechumenal Way by a lay artist, Francisco "Kiko" Argüello, and Carmen Hernández, who was from an industrialist family and a graduate of the Misioneras de Cristo Jesús Institute.[17] Following a highly successful model for the institutional establishment of the new ecclesial groups, Kiko Argüello and Carmen Hernández arrived in Rome in 1968 to open a center for the Way in the parish of Canadian Martyrs. The new movement's transfer to Rome led to the Way's early recognition, accompanied by an indication of adopting a more appropriate name—*Neocatechumenate*—for the path of catechesis of already-baptized adults, along the lines of the *Ordo initiationis christianae adultorum*, issued in 1972. In the spring and summer of 1974, after a series of meetings with the leaders of the movement, which were held when the Way had already become widespread in many parishes in Rome and in various dioceses of Italy, the Congregation for Divine Worship issued the first of a long series of "comments" on the liturgical practices of the Neocatechumenal Way, encouraging that the Way be rooted in parish communities, and formulated a wish rather than an order that "the 'Communities' in the parishes be built under the direction of the pastor."

It was the beginning of a long history of difficult relations between the Holy See and the bishops on one side and the Way on the other, especially because of the uniquely exclusive character of the Way's liturgical celebrations, which frequently led to tensions within the local churches and interventions by diocesan bishops. The pontificate of John Paul II had a soothing effect on the difficult relationship between Rome and the Way, but not quite in the same way as it had for other movements. On August 30, 1990, rather than recognizing the Neocatechumenal Way as an Association of the Faithful, the pope recognized the Way's "itinerary of formation," and Bishop Cordes was appointed *ad personam* to follow its apostolate. The new millennium brought *ad experimentum* approval of the Statutes of the Neocatechumenal Way for a five-year period; it was published on June 29, 2002, after the request was made by the movement during the audience granted by John Paul II on January 24, 1997, with the founders and leaders of the Neocatechumenal communities around the world.[18]

How much the Neocatechumenal communities are rooted in Italy is difficult to investigate, as are their public relations model and the underlying ecclesiological practice of movement. However, even an evaluation of the contribution of the Way to the implementation of Vatican II can proceed only by assuming certain lines of interpretation, which all need to be verified. One characteristic is clear and is common to both the Way's community life and the overall balance of its implementation of the Council, namely the centrality of the liturgy in the creation of its communitarian and spiritual identity.[19] It is no coincidence that the founders of the movement have given special attention to the aesthetic/artistic dimension of the communities and of the liturgies within the community, as it is indicative of the fact that the Congregation for Divine Worship was the first body from Rome to enter into dialogue with the movement and that it was on the liturgy that objections were focused—both by diocesan bishops and by the Holy See—regarding the movement's ecclesiology and its position in the Church, both at the local and universal level. The kerygmatic-catechetical synthesis of the Way focuses on a liturgical experience concentrating on the formative and theological training of the members of the movement. It begins as a journey of adult faith formation, and this new experience is based on a postbaptismal catechumenate, mediated through the threefold "word of God-liturgy-community" and in different stages (the kerygmatic, precatechumenate, catechumenate, and election stages), on the concept of the parish as a "community of communities" and on the internal structuring of the catechumenal community according to different services, all of which are entrusted to laypeople (leaders, local and itinerant catechists, cantors, readers, doorkeepers).

This centrality of a particular kind of liturgical experience for the Neocatechumenal Way is thus one of the problematic aspects of the implementation of Vatican II in Italy: that is, a liturgical renewal "spurred on" in some communities that are characterized by high spiritual and experiential intensity and by a difficult relationship with the local church, and an implementation of liturgical reform that is more dutiful but standardized and often stiff and complacent in the context of "local" parishes. In this sense, the (so far) brief history of the Way shows once again the centrality of the liturgical issue in the implementation of Vatican II and the problematic integration into local churches of a "liturgy-oriented movement" (but animated by a sensitivity that is quite different from the ecumenical rapprochement of the liturgical movement of the first half of the twentieth century).[20]

It seems clear that in a local church, such as in Italy, implementing liturgical reform was one of the problematic issues of the implementation of Vatican II: enough to provide the pretext for an anticonciliar kind of liturgical traditionalism launched against Vatican II, and stir up now-distant memories of the liturgical experimentation and ephemeral theological trends that held sway in the first period after the Council.[21] In this context, the Neocatechumenal Way presented the Church in Italy with a particular challenge: this movement's liturgical culture cannot be accused of rubricism or of rejection of the liturgical reform but, instead, threatened to interpret the liturgical reform in a strictly communitarian sense that was never in the mind of the Council fathers.

CATHOLIC CHARISMATIC RENEWAL

The Neocatechumenal Way was the most obvious example, but not the only one, of the vitality of the Catholic community even within the postconciliar Church.[22] Another movement that began in the United States at that time was also similarly disinterested regarding issues of institutional reform within the Church as a structure: the Charismatic Renewal. This movement, however, took a polar opposite position compared to the Neocatechumenal Way, in terms of ecumenical sensitivity (the United States had a Catholic minority, unlike Spain, which was overwhelmingly populated by Catholics and former Catholics) and the social and confessional geography from which it sprang (an active student environment in academic institutions with great intellectual prestige).

After a period of community meetings and contact with some *cursillistas* at the University of Notre Dame from 1964 to 1966, the movement was started on the East Coast between late 1966 and January 1967—from Pennsylvania, Indiana, and Michigan (Duquesne University in Pittsburgh; Notre Dame University in South Bend, Indiana; and the University of Michigan in Ann Arbor) to Iowa and Oregon. The Catholic Charismatic Renewal was based on ushering in a "renewed outpouring of the Holy Spirit" and on the rediscovery of baptismal grace and Christian identity.

In a movement whose founder is identified as the Holy Spirit and where charisms are manifold (charisms of renewed vigor, prophecy, intercession, healing, liberation, evangelization, and leadership), members seek charismatic spirituality, rather than a specific charism, and community dimension is a function of the dynamics among three aspects: "the flow of grace, existence as an ecclesial movement, and the status of private association of the faithful." The movement sees its theological basis as

> essentially trinitarian, according to the vision of the Church laid out by the Second Vatican Council in *Lumen Gentium*, particularly in a person's progressive knowledge of the Holy Spirit and his unhindered and irreplaceable action in the Church and in each of us.[23]

The first leaders of the Charismatic movement in the United States were anything but disembodied spiritualists, and were involved in the struggle for civil rights and intent on bringing "progressive" theologians such as Hans Küng onto the Notre Dame campus.[24] The Second Vatican Council was not in the foreground in the meetings of the movement, engaged as they were in charismatic prayer and in the creation of the community on the basis of specific Scripture passages (such as Acts 2—4), but the actual life of the first Catholic Charismatics was not all that far from the Council's call to ecumenism.[25]

From American universities, the movement spread through parishes and dioceses, led by priests and religious from different orders. At Notre Dame in the spring of 1968, the first community home of the movement, True House, was founded and became an important center for the activity of Charismatic Catholics. In 1969, again at Notre Dame, the first national meeting of Charismatic Catholics was held, gathering five hundred representatives from almost all of the United States. In 1970, the movement founded the *New Covenant Journal*, and in 1973, the first Directory of Catholic Prayer Groups was published. In 1976, the international office moved to Belgium, where it enjoyed the support of Cardinal Suenens. In Italy in 1971, thanks to Fr. Valerian Gaudet, the movement reached the Pontifical Gregorian University. In 1972, Charismatic Renewal came to Italy, where it developed progressively, away from the spotlight, but also guided in its growth by the interventions of the Church hierarchy.[26] More than other movements, in fact, the Renewal was influenced by the contribution of ecclesiastics who were not immediately involved in the experience, but gradually attracted to the spirituality lived out in it, not least because of the harmony of some of the movement's themes with the need for renewal that had been expressed by the Council. This is the case with Belgian Cardinal Leon-Joseph Suenens, one of the most influential leaders of Vatican II, who was contacted by members of the movement between 1971 and 1972, until (invited by the Jesuit Harold Cohen) he took part in the meeting in Notre Dame in June 1973, at which twenty-three thousand people from twenty-five countries participated.[27]

In 1969, the Doctrinal Commission of the US Bishops Conference accepted the movement, not least for the fact that according to Vatican II, "the spirit is always active in the church."[28] In 1969, after the first acknowledgment by the Catholic hierarchy of the existence of Charismatic Catholics, a "normalization" of the movement was made possible by the recognition accorded in two speeches by Paul VI while meeting with the leaders, on October 10, 1973, at the conference in Grottaferrata and on May 19, 1975, for Pentecost, after a series of cautious speeches by the pope (from 1967 onward) on Catholicism's need for Charismatic Renewal.[29]

The theological work of Suenens with leaders of the movement and his mediation with the pope between 1972 and 1975 seems to have been crucial.[30]

The Catholic Charismatic movement began in the United States as a latecomer to the charismatic renewal that was emerging from Protestant America, in a context of lived ecumenism that was not mediated by the official bilateral commissions chaired by the clergy of their respective churches. Once the movement arrived in Europe and in Italy, specifically, this nonconfessional (or nondenominational) aspect of the Renewal diminished, not so much because of specific choices made by the movement, but because it came into contact with a confessional geography that was radically different from that of North America. But since Vatican II, the Catholic Charismatic experience had conceived of the possibility of existing within the Church:

> Today the dichotomy between institution and charism is being gradually healed over....In the Second Vatican Council we have a remarkable instance of a reform council equally concerned about the authentic faith-life of persons and correct church order. In this prevailing atmosphere it is to be hoped that a movement such as charismatic renewal will be able to exist fruitfully within the institutional structure while at the same time serving and contributing to the renewal of the church.[31]

It is difficult to evaluate how deeply Charismatics are rooted in Italy, in the absence of reliable studies. One indicator of Italy's resistance to the Charismatic movement, at least for the first few years, can perhaps be traced to the fact that the first Italian member to join the International Liaison Committee was Hermes Ferrari in 1983, more than ten years after the arrival of the first groups in Italy.[32] As for how Vatican II was received, the tradition of the Catholic Renewal was begun with the Council, but avoided dealing directly with the legacy of Vatican II and instead focused on an exuberant internal community life dedicated to prayer and to the training and education of the members rather than to "public" theological reflection on issues of conciliar theology and pastoral work. In this sense, the relationship of the Catholic Charismatic movement with theology and public debate in the Church is typical of the whole phenomenon of the post–Vatican II movements.

CATHOLIC SCOUT MOVEMENT

The case of Catholic Scouting is of particular interest in the study of how the movements implemented the Council. Fidelity to the Second Vatican Council, in Italy and in France,[33] was in fact the origin of a lasting split between the anticonciliar wing of the Catholic Scout Movement (which was close to the traditionalist sentiments of Archbishop Marcel Lefebvre) and those who were more determined to adapt the new theological guidelines of "conciliar culture" (and of the Council as such) to educational, social, and liturgical initiatives.[34]

One particular example of development that is partly equivalent to what happened in Italy is that of French Catholic Scouting. The French Catholic Scout association reacted to the preconciliar crisis of the late fifties with a series of reforms, during the years of Vatican II, aimed at absorbing the new ecclesiology of the relationship between the Church and the world: the Catholic Boy Scout was no longer seen as a "crusader" in the fight against worldliness, but as a "citizen of the world." But in the years immediately following the end of Vatican II, the Scouts de France experienced a severe crisis, with leaders leaving the movement and membership declining. The situation worsened in 1968, with a number of splits toward the anticonciliar and traditionalist "right wing" (Scouts d'Europe, Scouts unitaire de France), which afflicted the movement right up to 1974. The end of the seventies marked the redefinition of the Scouts de France around a more consciously conciliar ecclesial identity, until in 1980, the movement met with Pope John Paul II in Bourget. Although the traditionalist association Scouts d'Europe (which in 1983 asked for canonical recognition as a lay association) challenged "the spirit of the Council" and not the Council as such, it is no coincidence that Archbishop Marcel Lefebvre's France harbored the most conservative wing of the Catholic Scouting movement, where—at least up to the

beginning of the twenty-first century—its numerically most rele- ·
vant and ideologically more energetic core could still be found.[35]

Italy's case, however, is interesting because it shows an integral
and courageous implementation of the Council, but at the same
time it is almost omitted (compared to the French case) from the
studies on pastoral theology and the sociology of the contemporary
Italian church.[36] With a methodology partly indebted to the founder
of the World Scout Movement, the Englishman Lord Robert Baden-
Powell (1857–1941), and in part to the language of the Franco-
Belgian Young Christian Workers (JOC—Jeunesse Ouvrière
Chrétienne), the Italian version of the Catholic Scouting movement
was from the beginning quite marked by its "ecclesial character" and
its "rivalry" with Catholic Action, which remained hegemonic right
up to the Council and beyond in its privileged relationship with the
bishops and the Holy See.[37] Having recovered after the abolition of
the Associazione Scautistica Cattolica Italiana (ASCI) by the Fascist
regime in 1928 and becoming ever stronger in the years of rivalry
with the "green berets" of Luigi Gedda, the leader of Catholic Action
in Italy, the Italian Catholic Scouting movement implemented the
Council on the basis of its strong roots in Northern Italy and Lombardy (where illegal scouting groups had existed illegally even under
the Fascist regime).[38]

For a long time, the Italian Catholic Scout movement was
able to manage the mixture between a language and a symbolism
that was still largely paramilitary, flavored with the rhetoric of
honor and loyalty, with the antiauthoritarian impulses of the seventies, and was not immune to the scope of the new teachings of
the Council. From the first half of the seventies, the autonomy of
Catholic scouting (and especially of the female wing of the movement, AGI/Associazione Guide Italiane) from Church hierarchy
resulted not only in the ostentatious coldness of Catholic Scouts
regarding the bishops' "call to arms" (for example in the referendum against the law introducing divorce in Italy in 1974) for Italian Catholic laity, but also in a clear reluctance to answer every call
of the bishops for the "political unity of Italian Catholics" in the
context of national elections. All this also resulted in a relationship
with the local church that showed Catholic Scouts' greater autonomy from the bishops and pastors, compared to the umbilical cord
typical of Catholic Action and other postconciliar bodies: not only

in the selection of leaders through an election mechanism, but also regarding the participation of Catholic Scouts in pastoral (or political) initiatives, whether at the diocesan or national level.

In 1974, the part of the Italian Catholic Scouting movement that was most faithful to Vatican II and more politically aware to the challenges of the time (in the spirit of Don Milani's motto *I care*) was to merge the female association, AGI, with its male counterpart, ASCI, in order to form the new AGESCI (Associazione Guide e Scout Cattolici Italiani). In Italy, the year 1974 marks the beginning of a long period of domestic terrorism, and Italian Catholic laity was part of the picture of a country in a deep political crisis. Marked by a progressive political culture that was programmatically democratic and antifascist, and by a relationship of loyalty to the Catholic Church—but without the direct hierarchical obedience of Catholic Action—AGESCI's statutes were defined an "association-movement" that transformed a theological and political option into commitment to education of the youth. The "covenant," the foundational text of the Italian Catholic scout association closely tied together the "scouting choice" (scouting as an educational method), "political choice" (which was nonpartisan, but geared to active participation and responsible for the realization of the common good), and "Christian choice "(to live and witness within the Catholic Church) in a spirit of shared bond of association with the sociopolitical community and with the Christian community.

During the eighties, the Catholic Scout movement's theological loyalty to the legacy of Vatican II deepened. The publication of the *Progetto unitario di Catechesi* (Catechetical Unified Project, 1983) developed AGESCI's commitment as an agency of educators in the faith, formally incorporated into the pastoral work of the local church and professing an ecclesiology of the local church and the practice of the laity (by the educators) that already acknowledged the end of the model of "ecclesiastical assistant" to whom spiritual formation could be delegated. The national meeting of the thousands of members (sixteen to twenty-one years old), in the summer of 1986, was host to John Paul II[39] and launched the association into its period of greatest expansion, culminating in the national meeting for community training leaders in the summer of 1997, which had as its theme a reflection on the educator as a protagonist in the Church or in the civil community, with references made that were not quite explicit but applicable to the figure of the politician and later monk Giuseppe Dossetti (who had died just a few months before, in December 1996), a key figure for Italian Catholicism in the twentieth century and especially for his role at Vatican II and in post–Vatican II Catholicism.[40]

The implementation of Vatican II by Italian Catholic Scouts—who were almost totally immune to the phenomena of anticonciliar or preconciliar intolerance[41]—took place in a particular way in the context of the new ecclesial movements. In fact, the significant growth in numbers of AGESCI during the eighties and nineties (in contrast with other movements within Catholicism overall) corresponds to their choice to manage themselves on a membership, democratic, and participatory basis, and was characterized by a lively internal political pluralism, but without yearning after a submission to the Italian bishops—as it was typical of other movements, especially concerning political issues.

AGESCI scouting has primarily practiced a cultural and theological interpretation of Vatican II with involvement from leading figures of the Italian church: Fr. Lorenzo Milani (for his ability to dampen down the military symbolism of scouting); Giuseppe Dossetti, the partisan and monk (for uniting civic commitment and church ministry); and Jesuit Cardinal Carlo Maria Martini (for promoting the word of God in the life of the lay faithful, closely linked to some of the experiences of the Bible camps in Italy[42]). In addition to these prominent figures, Italian Catholic Scout movement chose as reference points circles and traditions that most express the deep roots of some of the leaders of Italian Catholic scouting in Milan and Lombardy (Fr. Giorgio Basadonna[43]) and their closeness to the biblical spirituality of some neomonastic communities (Taizé, the Community of Bose), rather than a real continuity with Italian Catholicism in dioceses and parishes, more typical of Catholic Action. This mixture between the venerable traditions of the now century-old scouting method and the ability to update the language with a biblical spirituality is probably the strength of the Italian Catholic Scout movement in its interpretation of Vatican II; the weakness of the "Scouting for Boys" method, in trying to filter Vatican II beyond the confines of the association, is to be found in its relative inability to make its voice heard within the institution of the Church, even with such a large number of members that should outweigh the strength of other new and more aggressive Catholic movements.

CATHOLIC MOVEMENTS AND THE IMPLEMENTATION OF THE COUNCIL: SOME CONCLUSIONS

A first element of interest in the particular history of the international Catholic movements in Italy in the postconciliar period concerns the comparison between the characteristics of these new movements and, more generally, how we go about studying the implementation of Vatican II, the first truly global Council, among those movements as global movements of the one Catholic Church. A first lesson to be drawn is methodological, about the way to interpret them, which must remain much more intrinsic to the development of their various expressions and associative traditions, as far as possible, given the relative impossibility or uselessness of following their progression in comparison with the development of the implementation of Vatican II as part of the religious history of a particular local church. In fact, it is true that for Italian Catholicism, the immediate postconciliar period and the climate in 1968 constituted a breeding ground for the new movements. But it was also the beginning of the "big sort" among many groups and ecclesial associations, especially around the issue of the relationship between faith communities and political commitment; this interpretation, however, can hardly be applied to movements that had an international presence.

A second element concerns these international movements' trajectories and strategies for implementing Vatican II or for taking a particular approach to (or distance from) Vatican II in a given situation. Within the movements, there was a place for "spontaneous implementation" of Vatican II in the broad sense—through an experience of the Council coming through the mass media, reading the final documents, and a general change in the cultural and theological climate. In these international ecclesial aggregations, the dynamics of implementation were less conditioned than for European entities that were closer to the tradition of Catholic Action: the liberating condition was the freedom from the need to come up with an effective response to the dramatic crisis of preconciliar Catholic associations in the postconciliar period. This is the case for charismatic groups, which do not have to deal with the heavy cultural and organizational baggage of an association that developed in the Church in the first half of the twentieth century and can, in a few years, shape a spiritual culture that is independent from both the culture of "crisis of civilization" of the 1930s and from the debate around the issue of the newness of the Council as a turning point or as a "rupture."

Nevertheless, the development of these international movements is sometimes the projection on a European and global scale of spiritual models and associative cultures that arose in a certain context of European Christendom and were exported elsewhere with no little success (as with the Focolare and the Neocatechumenal Way). On the other hand, it is also apparent how the dynamics of the local churches influenced the international movements and embedded themselves in the development of their implementation of Vatican II and how similar spiritual cultures express themselves and divide around the question of implementing the Council (as in the parallel cases of the Italian and French Scouting movements).

A third issue concerns the relationship between the numerical size of international movements and their method of implementation. The most obvious difference between experiences like that of a mass organization like Catholic Scout movement (at the end of the 1990s almost two hundred thousand members in Italy alone) on the one hand, and Opus Dei, the Neocatechumenal Way, and Sant'Egidio (for example) on the other, concerned their numbers. While, on the one hand, there are "associations-movements" such as Catholic Action and the Catholic Scout movement, which included tens of thousands of members between adults and children, on the other hand, there are associations with a lower rate of institutionalization that have not only chosen a framework of much lighter (or much less formal and visible) associative and organizational structures, but that were directed at a Catholic elite made up of niches and members from the cultural, intellectual, and spiritual avant-garde. From this point of view, in the period between Pope Paul VI's pontificate and the end of John Paul II's, the ability of the "new ecclesial movements" to influence the institutional complex of the Catholic Church and to accompany it on its postconciliar path has been often inversely proportional to their size, to the democratic nature of their political culture, and to their rate of institutionalization and bureaucratization. In this sense, the international development of the movements did not appear to compromise this characteristic of "institutional lightness," which together with their implementation of Vatican II—transmitted through charismatic leadership rather than through a "democratic" coming together of their members—constitutes the key to their success.

A fourth element is the relationship between conciliar implementation among the movements and a particular religious geography. Italian religious geography, in the sense of a spiritual landscape, allows or fuels a certain type of development among the movements in Italian churches. There is a difference between the theological matrix of those movements that "intensify" and develop a charism derived from Catholic Action (including the Catholic Scout movement) and those movements with origins in a multiconfessional environment (such as the Charismatic Renewal) or with an intrinsic ecumenical vocation (such as the Focolare): their impact with a confessional geography and an Italian spiritual landscape that is uniformly Catholic or post-Catholic produces different models of presence in the Italian Catholic Church. In this sense, it would be helpful to have a census of how embedded in dioceses movements are (especially in diocesan pastoral councils, diocesan synods, and seminaries), in order to assess not only the presence of the movements in the territory of the local churches, but also their inclusion within the church institutions that are most affected by the postconciliar reforms.[44]

The issue of movements, in fact, appears central to a comprehensive appreciation of the implementation of Vatican II, both by the Church and by the observers of the evolution of Catholicism as a worldwide phenomenon, in a time when Catholicism seems to have hope for the future only from the latitudes of the global south.[45]

But in "old Europe" in recent times, some controversies that have resounded within the sphere of ecclesial public opinion have suggested, as the key to understanding the postconciliar tensions between local churches and the Roman See, a polarity between Catholic movements (defenders of the pope as the voice of the universality of the Catholic Church) and "ecclesial regionalism" (which can be understood as a vociferous representation of local churches aimed at the government of the universal Church by the Roman See).[46] The image of the local churches as a mirror of a "ecclesial regionalism," even if a little hasty on the ecclesiological level, has its merits and is not devoid of interest, especially from the point of view of the history of relations between the papacy and the local churches (especially non-Italian ones).[47] From the point of view of the history of the implementation of Vatican II, in Italy, which sees within its borders "Catholic churches in Italy" rather than "the Italian Catholic Church," the phenomenon of the movements that have a major international presence can provide elements of reflection for understanding the specific nature of implementation of Vatican II in a country that many have considered the backyard of the Vatican. In this sense, given the particular role of Rome and Italy in the spiritual geography and in the geopolitics of Roman Catholicism, the path of the new ecclesial movements in Italy is more than just one case study among many others.

Notes

1. For a comprehensive study of the issue, please refer to Massimo Faggioli, *Sorting Out Catholicism: A Brief History of the New Ecclesial Movements* (Collegeville, MN: Liturgical Press, 2014).

2. For the implementation of Vatican II, see the studies by Gilles Routhier, from *La Réception d'un Concile* (Paris: Cerf, 1993), to *Cinquante ans après Vatican II* (Paris: Cerf, 2014).

3. Massimo Faggioli, "Between Documents and Spirit: The Case of the New Catholic Movements," in *After Vatican II: Trajectories and Hermeneutics*, ed. James L. Heft with John O'Malley (Grand Rapids: Eerdmans, 2012), 1–22.

4. See *Vatican II: Did Anything Happen?* ed. David G. Schultenover (New York: Continuum, 2007); John W. O'Malley, *What Happened at Vatican II* (Cambridge, MA: Belknap Press of Harvard University Press, 2008); Massimo Faggioli, *Vatican II: The Battle for Meaning* (New York: Paulist Press, 2012).

5. For an extensive reflection on Catholicism and the "secular age," see Charles Taylor, *A Secular Age* (Cambridge, MA: Belknap Press of Harvard University Press, 2007).

6. See Massimo Faggioli, "Tra chiesa territoriale e chiese personali. I movimenti ecclesiali nel post-concilio Vaticano II," in *I movimenti nella storia del cristianesimo. Caratteristiche—variazioni—continuità*. Special issue of *Cristianesimo nella Storia*, ed. Giuseppe Alberigo and Massimo Faggioli, 24, no. 3 (2003): 677–704.

7. See Daniela Saresella, *Dal Concilio alla contestazione. Riviste cattoliche negli anni del cambiamento (1958–1968)* (Brescia: Morcelliana, 2005).

8. See *Fedeli, associazioni, movimenti*, ed. the Group of Italian teachers of Canon Law (Milan: Glossa, 2002); Eugenio Corecco, "Profili istituzionali dei movimenti nella Chiesa," in *Ius et Communio. Scritti di diritto canonico*, vol. 2 (Casale Monferrato: Theology Faculty of Lugano, 1997), 143–74; Barbara Zadra, *I movimenti ecclesiali e i loro statute* (Rome: Pontificia Università Gregoriana, 1997).

9. In the case of Opus Dei, between 1960 and January 1962, Escrivà de Balaguer asked the Holy See to transform the Opus Dei from a secular institution to a *prelature nullius*, with a structure parallel to that of *Mission de France*; neither Paul VI nor John XXIII granted Opus Dei's request. In 1969, Paul VI invited Opus Dei to hold a general congress in order to investigate the issues related to the nature of their work. But the demand for recognition was only revived in 1979, that is, after the end of Pope Paul's pontificate. See Giancarlo Rocca, *L'Opus Dei. Appunti e documenti per una storia* (Milan: Paoline, 1985).

10. There are many works that map out the progression of existing movements, and there is a very large bibliography on the subject: Jesús Castellano Cervera, *Carismi per il terzo millennio. I movimenti ecclesiali e le nuove comunità* (Rome: OCD, 2001); *Movimenti ecclesiali contemporanei. Dimensioni storiche, teologico-spirituali ed apostoliche*, ed. Agostino Favale, 4th ed. (Rome: LAS, 1991); Agostino Favale, *Segni di vitalità nella Chiesa. Movimenti e nuove comunità* (Rome: LAS, 2009); Antonio Giolo and Brunetto Salvarani, *I cattolici sono tutti uguali? Una mappa dei movimenti della Chiesa* (Genoa: Marietti, 1992); *I movimenti della Chiesa negli anni Ottanta* (Milan: Jaca Book, 1982); *I movimenti nella chiesa. Atti del II colloquio internazionale: Vocazione e missione dei laici nella chiesa oggi* (Milan: Nuovo Mondo, 1987); *Lebenswege des Glaubens: Berichte über Mönchtum heute, Gemeinschaften Charles de Foucaulds, Fokolar-Bewegung, Gemeinschaften christlichen Lebens, Schönstatt-Bewegung, Équipes Notre-Dame*, ed. Joseph Sauer (Freiburg i.B.: Herder, 1978); Bruno Secondin, *I nuovi pro-

.*tagonisti, movimenti, associazioni, gruppi nella Chiesa* (Cinisello Balsamo: Paoline, 1991).

11. On the implementation of Vatican II in Italy, see *Il Vaticano II in Emilia Romagna. Apporti e ricezioni*, ed. Maurizio Tagliaferri (Bologna: EDB, 2007).

12. See Christoph Hegge, *Rezeption und Charisma. Der theologische und rechtliche Beitrag Kirchlicher Bewegungen zur Rezeption des Zweiten Vatikanische Konzils* (Würzburg: Echter, 1999); Christoph Hegge, *Il Vaticano II e i movimenti ecclesiali: una recezione carismatica* (Rome: Città Nuova, 2001).

13. See Enzo M. Fondi, Michele Zanzucchi, *Un popolo nato dal Vangelo. Chiara Lubich e i Focolari* (Cinisello Balsamo: San Paolo, 2003), mostly based on Igino Giordani's *Storia del movimento dei Focolari*, mimeograph, 3 vols. (Rocca di Papa, 1977); Chiara Lubich and Igino Giordani, *"Erano i tempi di guerra..." Agli albori dell'ideale dell'unità* (Rome: Città Nuova, 2007), with part of it dedicated to "the history of the emerging Focolari movement," 41–228.

14. See Chiara Lubich, *L'avventura dell'unità* (Rome: Paoline, 1991).

15. Cf. Edwin Robertson, *The Fire of Love: A Life of Igino Giordani, "Foco," 1894–1980* (London: New City, 1989).

16. The Focolare movements claim to be currently present in 182 countries, 89 of them with permanent centers, as follows: Europe (29), Africa (25), America (19), Asia (13) Oceania (3).

17. See Kiko Argüello, "Le comunità neocatecumenali," *Rivista di vita spirituale* 2 (1975); Bernard Sven Anuth, *Der Neokatechumenale Weg: Geschichte, Erscheinungsbild, Rechtscharakter* (Würzburg: Echter, 2006); Ricardo Blazquez, *Le comunità neocatecumenali. Discernimento teologico*, ed. Ezechiele Pasotti (Cinisello B.: San Paolo, 1995); Paolo Sorci, "Ermeneutica della Parola nel cammino neocatecumenale," *Rivista liturgica* 84, no. 6 (1997): 867–80.

18. With the delivery of the formal decree of approval from the president of the Pontifical Council for the Laity to Kiko Argüello and Carmen Hernández, the founders of the Way and to Fr. Mario Pezzi, the legal process, which had started in 2002, came to an end on June 13, 2008, when the text of the statutes was approved *ad experimentum*.

19. For a different view on the centrality of the liturgy in the implementation of Vatican II, see Massimo Faggioli, *True Reform: Liturgy and Ecclesiology in Sacrosanctum Concilium* (Collegeville, MN: Liturgical Press, 2012).

20. Cf. Raymond Loonbeek and Jacques Mortiau, *Un pionnier, Dom*

Lambert Beauduin (1873–1960). Liturgie et unité des chrétiens, 2 vols. (Louvain-la-Neuve: Collège Erasme, 2001).

21. See Alberto Melloni, "Il canto liturgico nella periferia della chiesa italiana: problemi e casi di studio," Musica e storia, 13, no. 3 (2005): 471–88.

22. See Paolo Maino, Il post-moderno nella Chiesa? Il Rinnovamento carismatico (Cinisello Balsamo: San Paolo, 2004); Mario Panciera, Il Rinnovamento nello spirito in Italia: una realtà ecclesiale (Rome: RnS, 1992); Francis A. Sullivan, Charisms and Charismatic Renewal: A Biblical and Theological Study (Ann Arbor, MI: Servant Books, 1982); Peter Zimmerling, Die charismatischen Bewegungen. Theologie—Spiritualität—Anstöße zum Gespräch (Göttingen: Vandenhoeck & Ruprecht, 2001).

23. Salvatore Martinez, address at the international seminar for bishops on "Ecclesial Movements in the Pastoral Care of Bishops" (Rome, June 18, 1999), http://www.rns-italia.it/vademecum/Vademecum.htm# IlRnSInItalia.

24. Edward O'Connor, Le renouveau charismatique: Origines et perspectives (Paris: Editions Beauchesne, 1975), esp. 221–96; Randy R. McGuire, "Catholic Charismatic Renewal: The Struggle for Affirmation (1967–1975)," PhD diss., Saint Louis University, 1998, esp. 100–104.

25. One of the first testimonies appears in Kevin and Dorothy Ranaghan, Catholic Pentecostals (Paramus, NJ: Paulist Press, 1969). Kevin Ranaghan was enrolled in the theology doctorate program at the University of Notre Dame, and his dissertation was on the liturgy. See Kilian McDonnell (one of the first leaders), The Charismatic Renewal and Ecumenism (New York: Paulist Press, 1978).

26. On March 14, 2002, on the thirtieth anniversary of its presence in the Italian church, Charismatic Renewal received from the Italian Bishops Conference approval of its statute; the decision was announced by Cardinal Camillo Ruini (president of the Italian bishops) in his homily in St. John Lateran on the occasion of the thirtieth anniversary of the presence of the Renewal in Italy.

27. See Leon-Joseph Suenens, Memories and Hopes (Dublin: Veritas, 1992).

28. See McGuire, "Catholic Charismatic Renewal," 287–89.

29. See Presence, Power, Praise: Documents on the Charismatic Renewal, ed. Kilian McDonnell, 3 vols. (Collegeville, MN: Liturgical Press, 1980).

30. On the declarations of Grottaferrata and of Malines (1974), see Leon-Joseph Suenens, A New Pentecost? (New York: Seabury Press, 1975).

31. Kevin and Dorothy Ranaghan, *Catholic Pentecostals Today* (South Bend, IN: Charismatic Renewal Services, 1983), 189.

32. See http://www.iccrs.org/about.php.

33. See Madeleine Bourcereau, *Jacques Sevin, fondateur et mystique: 1882–1951* (Paris: Salvator, 2007).

34. See *Le scoutisme: quel type d'homme? Quel type de femme? Quel type de chrétien?* ed. Gerard Cholvy et Marie-Thérèse Cheroutre (Paris: Cerf, 1994).

35. See Gerard Cholvy, *Histoire des organisations et mouvements chrétiens de jeunesse en France, XIXe–XXe siècle* (Paris: Cerf, 1999) 338–68; Marie-Thérèse Cheroutre, *Le Scoutisme au féminin. Les Guides de France, 1923–1998* (Paris: Cerf, 2002); Christian Guérin, *L'utopie Scouts de France. Histoire d'une identité collective, catholique et sociale 1920–1995* (Paris: Fayard, 1997); Philippe Laneyrie, *Les Scouts de France. L'évolution du Mouvement des origines aux annés 80* (Paris: Cerf, 1985).

36. There are various volumes of local history of the Italian Scout movement, which are interesting as sources but are mostly celebratory. Even the most solid and authoritative studies have an "internal" bias regarding the Italian Scouting movement: Mario Sica, *Storia dello scautismo in Italia* (Florence: La Nuova Italia, 1973; Rome: Fiordaliso, 2006); Vincenzo Schirripa, *Giovani sulla frontiera. Guide e Scout cattolici nell'Italia repubblicana (1943–1974)* (Rome: Studium, 2006).

37. See Paola Dal Toso, *Nascita e diffusione dell'ASCI 1916–1928* (Milan: Franco Angeli, 2007).

38. The boys from the Scout groups in Milan and Monza called themselves *Stray Eagles,* and they performed clandestine activities during the period of Fascism after the dissolution of the Scouts decreed by the regime in 1928 (one year before Mussolini and Pius XI signed the Lateran Treaty that put to an end the "Roman question" and gave the pope Vatican City State).

39. For a significant sociological analysis of the guidelines of the Catholic Scouting movement in the mid-eighties, see *Scouts oggi. Diecimila rovers scolte dell'AGESCI rispondono* (Rome: Borla, 1989). For the speeches of John Paul II to young AGESCI members on that occasion (August 9, 1986), which focused on the "spirituality of scouting," see *Documenti pontifici sullo scoutismo,* ed. Giovanni Morello and Francesco Pieri (Milan: Ancora, 1991) 289–97.

40. See *Giuseppe Dossetti: Studies on an Italian Catholic Reformer,* ed. Alberto Melloni (Berlin: LIT, 2008).

41. The impact of theological traditionalism on the Catholic Scout movement is limited, even considering the limited impact in Italy of the traditionalist "Scouts of Europe" association, the most conservative wing

of Italian Catholic Scouting, which, however, in the years of Benedict XVI, received some symbolic signs of recognition from the Holy See.

42. See the experience of "Bible Camps," created by Agnese Cini Tassinario, then founder of the Biblia association: see *Come la pioggia e la neve...: Storie ed emozioni dai 35 anni dei Campi Bibbia Agesci*, ed. Francesco Chiulli and Maria Teresa Spagnoletti (Rome: Scout AGESCI-Fiordaliso, 2006).

43. About Fr. Giorgio Basadonna (1922–2008), see his best-selling book on the spirituality of the road, *Spiritualità della strada* (Milan: Ancora, 1979, republished several times).

44. For an interesting study on this area that covers the case of the French church, *Le gouvernement de l'église catholique. Synodes et exercice du pouvoir*, ed. Jacques Palard (Paris: Cerf, 1997).

45. See Philip Jenkins, *The Next Christendom: The Coming of Global Christianity* (Oxford: Oxford University Press, 2002).

46. "The Church, and the various local Churches, are struggling to stay united. There is a phenomenon of real 'ecclesial regionalism.' The fact is that, paradoxically, in the era of globalization the world has been simultaneously broken into its various national and religious identities. Today it is very difficult to grow a global vision within the Church, even though it is such by its very nature." From the interview with Andrea Riccardi (founder of the Community of Sant'Egidio) by Maria Antoinetta Calabrò, in *Corriere della Sera*, March 24, 2009.

47. See Massimo Faggioli, "Chiese locali ed ecclesiologia prima e dopo il concilio di Trento," in *Storia della Chiesa in Europa tra ordinamento politico-amministrativo e strutture ecclesiastiche*, ed. Luciano Vaccaro (Brescia: Morcelliana, 2005) 197–213.

5

VATICAN II BETWEEN DOCUMENTS AND SPIRIT

The Case of the "New Catholic Movements"

T HE CENTRAL PLACE of the new Catholic movements in the contemporary Catholic Church has to be addressed from the point of view of their historical origins and relationship with Vatican II. That is what I propose to do here. By new Catholic movements, I mean, of course, such institutions as Communion and Liberation, the Community of Sant'Egidio, Focolare, Neo-catechumenal Way, Cursillos de Cristiandad, and the Regnum Christi movement of the Legionaries of Christ.

It is indeed common to speak of these movements as "the fruit of Vatican II." Indeed, the movements tend to define themselves that way. Although not without basis, that definition raises questions about just how they are the fruit of the Council and, more specifically, how they relate to the major issues-under-the-issues to which John O'Malley called our attention. Among those issues, I will concentrate on the relationship between center and periphery, but as O'Malley points out, the issues are intertwined, so that dealing with one entails dealing in some measure with the others.

It is not easy to categorize these movements, but it is clear that both their auto-definitions and the description of them in the Code of Canon Law are of little help. The minimum common characteristics can be summarized as follows: a group of Catholics who have

> a charismatic founder, a particular charism, some form of ecclesial reality or expression, a predominantly lay membership, a radical commitment to the Gospel, a form of teaching or training closely linked to its charism, a specific focus and a commitment to bringing its own emphasis or understanding into the life of the Church.[1]

These new movements, which presuppose a stable commitment and a rule to follow, which may be written or customary, have often been pegged as integralist, fundamentalist, ultramontane, and sectarian. Hard feelings are often the source of biased judgments in the debate about them. But as many of these movements were founded after Vatican II, they clearly are an integral part of the face of post–Vatican II Catholicism.

The question is thus not whether there is a relationship between the movements and Vatican II, but rather what kind of Vatican II they claim to be the fruit of: the literal meaning of the documents of Vatican II or the "spirit of Vatican II"? It is indeed necessary to investigate the relationship between the new Catholic movements and the allegedly distorting appeal to the "spirit of Vatican II" in order to explain and defend their success and role in the post–Vatican II Catholic Church.[2] This chapter will help us to understand that post–Vatican II Catholicism as well as the battle for control of the Council's legacy must be based on the narrative of the documents and its interpretation, given that "it is not the documents that reveal how hot the issue was but the narrative of the battles for control of the council itself."[3]

ECCLESIAL MOVEMENTS FROM THE "LONG NINETEENTH CENTURY" TO VATICAN II

A decisive element of the passage between the "long nine-teenth century," Vatican II, and the new Catholic movements was the contribution of the "revival movements" of the early twentieth century.[4] The biblical movement, the patristic revival and res-sourcement, the liturgical renewal, and the ecumenical movement based in Europe and North America had survived the modernist crisis at the beginning of the twentieth century[5] and the condem-nations of Pius XII, and had managed to bring the fathers and *periti* of Vatican II to the core of their historical-theological reflec-tions for the aggiornamento of the Catholic Church.[6]

The *biblical revival* introduced into the Catholic Church the drive for direct access to the Bible for the faithful, with emphasis on the importance of the historical-critical method of biblical scholarship, in order to give all Catholics the opportunity to reach the word of God in the Scripture and thus nourish their spiritual life.[7] The *liturgical renewal* stressed the need to reset the balance of the life of the Church around the liturgy and to renew liturgical language in order to strengthen the connection between spiritual life and the sources of liturgy, with liturgy itself as a source.[8] The *ecumenical movement* had suffered some severe setbacks from Rome from the 1920s on, but at the local level, it had slowly bro-ken the taboo on official relations between Catholics, Protestants, and Orthodox Christians.[9] The *patristic renewal* had advocated the return to the great tradition of the fathers of the Church.[10]

The Catholic Church arrived at the end of Pius XII's pon-tificate and on the eve of Vatican II in a complex situation: an extremely Rome-centered and Curia-controlled theology officially still based on Thomas Aquinas's guidelines for theological and spiritual identity held sway, while the revival or renewal move-ments were gaining audience in the theological and wider eccle-siastical milieu. These revival movements directly contributed to the Council debate on ecclesiology, which became the main issue debated at Vatican II. Nevertheless, the issue of the Catholic movements did not take center stage at Vatican II, either from a theological or a canonical point of view.

THE EVENT OF VATICAN II AND THE CATHOLIC MOVEMENTS

The new Catholic movements identify themselves as the real "fruit" of Vatican II,[11] encouraged by John Paul II, who repeatedly affirmed the relationship between the movements and Vatican II.[12] In fact, the event of Vatican II had a profound impact on the history of the organizations and movements of the Catholic laity, but the relationship between the Council and the identity of the new movements is far from direct and unequivocal.

John XXIII announced Vatican II on January 25, 1959, after Pius XII's long pontificate had confirmed and exalted, in continuity with Pius XI's intuition, Catholic Action as *the* organization of the Catholic laity in a still-Eurocentric Catholicism.[13] Although the fortunes of Catholic Action were different in the United States, it was crucial in other parts of the Catholic world, especially Western Europe, where it was the matrix of twentieth-century Catholic laity.[14] Pius XI's and Pius XII's strategic option for the presence of the Catholic Church in the European States at the crossroads of nationalistic ideologies (Fascism in Italy, Nazism in Germany) and the Communist threat (in Eastern Europe) was the creation of Catholic Action. Based on late nineteenth-century social Catholicism, every single group and community would be closely controlled by the pope, bishops, and clergy. In the Catholic Church of the first half of the twentieth century, Catholics officially had no room for autonomy in the political sphere or for the theological insights of the renewal movements (biblical, ecumenical, and liturgical). Within European Catholicism of the 1920s–40s, Catholic Action was supposed to educate the lay faithful, to "protect" them from the bad influences of the modern ideologies (both socialist-communist and nationalist-fascist) and to control every possible social, political, and theological "motion" of the *ecclesia discens*—the "learning Church"—carefully guided by the "teaching Church" and its supreme leader, the pope.

Within the walls of official Catholicism, however, Catholic Action managed to contain some seeds of the theological renewal movements as well as of the future leaders and insights of the new Catholic movements. The Council developed some aspects of the "theology of the laity" that was born in Europe in the 1940s.[15] The growth of the movements, however, was due to the identity crisis of Catholic Action. But the connection between Vatican II, its debates and final texts on one side, and the new Catholic movements on the other, is complex.

If we look at the history of Vatican II and the outcomes of the debates, it is clear that the Council did not directly address the issue of the newborn movements.[16] Vatican II debated some aspects of the life of the Catholic associations and of Catholic Action in particular, trying to revitalize the old cradles of Catholic lay elites with some injection of the French theology of the laity. The Council benefited from the experience of the reform movements (biblical, liturgical, ecumenical, patristic renewal), but the profound culture of those old renewal movements did not reach the core theological and spiritual identity of the new Catholic movements.

The documents of Vatican II provided the new movements with a general legitimacy for a new central place for the laity in the Church. This is especially true of the decree *Apostolicam Actuositatem* on the lay apostolate, chapter 4 of the constitution *Lumen Gentium* on the laity, the pastoral constitution *Gaudium et Spes* on the Church and the modern world (paragraph 43), and the decree *Presbyterorum Ordinis* (paragraph 8). Only *Apostolicam Actuositatem* directly addressed the issue of the organizations of the laity, mentioning no movement but Catholic Action.

Vatican II's approach to the issue of the lay apostolate was purely theological, with no attention given to the juridical, canonical, or institutional aspects of the organized movements (plural) supporting the new central position of the Catholic laity.[17] The debate on the floor and the commission of Vatican II that produced the schema *de apostolatu laicorum* focused on the need to clearly define the theological identity of the laity, that is, the rights, duties, and opportunities for the activity of the laity in the Church. The debate never went beyond the boundaries of a concept of the lay apostolate as "animation of temporal realities" in communion with the hierarchy of the Church.[18]

Chapter 4 of *Apostolicam Actuositatem*, whose title reads, "The Various Forms of the Apostolate," in paragraphs 18–21, and especially in paragraph 20, specifies the variety of the forms of the organized apostolate, the need for such an apostolate, and the risk of a dissipation of the lay apostolate's human resources. Paragraph 18 of the decree states the possibility to be an apostle "both in their family communities and in their parishes and dioceses, which themselves express the community nature of the apostolate, as well as in the informal groups which they decide to form among themselves." Paragraph 20 refers to Catholic Action, presented as the typical form of organized apostolate, and does not mention other kinds of associations and movements, even though it leaves some room for other solutions: "Organizations in which, in the opinion of the hierarchy, the ensemble of these characteristics is realized, must be considered to be Catholic Action even though they take on various forms and titles because of the needs of different regions and peoples." In particular, *Apostolicam actuositatem* tried to collect under Pius XI's ideal type of apostolate, that is, Catholic Action, a variety of associations and groups that were never able or willing to unite in a unique association:

> Whether these forms of the apostolate have the name of "Catholic Action" or some other title, they exercise an apostolate of great value for our times and consist in the combination and simultaneous possession of the following characteristics:
>
> a) The immediate aim of organizations of this kind is the Church's apostolic aim, that is, the evangelization and sanctification of men and the formation of a Christian conscience among them so that they can infuse the spirit of the Gospel into various communities and departments of life.
>
> b) Cooperating with the hierarchy in their own way, the laity contribute the benefit of their experience to, and assume responsibility for the direction of these

organizations, the consideration of the conditions in which the pastoral activity of the Church is to be conducted, and the elaboration and execution of the plan of things to be done.

c) The laity acts together in the manner of an organic body so that the community of the Church is more fittingly symbolized and the apostolate rendered more effective.

d) Whether they offer themselves spontaneously or are invited to action and direct cooperation with the apostolate of the hierarchy, the laity function under the higher direction of the hierarchy itself, and the latter can sanction this cooperation by an explicit mandate.[19]

It is easy to see how the documents of Vatican II maintained the concept of a lay apostolate next to the ideal of Catholic Action, slightly more independently of the ecclesiastical hierarchy but still in need of a mandate from the hierarchy. This element would soon fade in the post–Vatican II praxis of the Catholic movements, which featured a growing organizational independence (especially from the bishops and dioceses where they are active) and an increasingly advertised obedience to the pontifical magisterium. Yet the constitution *Lumen Gentium*, in chapter 2 on "The People of God," stressed the relationship between charisms and the judgment of the "appointed leaders of the Church":

The Holy Spirit...distributes special graces among the faithful of every rank. By these gifts He makes them fit and ready to undertake the various tasks and offices which contribute toward the renewal and building up of the Church, according to the words of the Apostle: "The manifestation of the Spirit is given to everyone for profit." These charisms, whether they be the more outstanding or the more simple and widely diffused, are to be received with thanksgiving and consolation for they are perfectly suited to and useful for the needs of the Church. Extraordinary gifts are not to be sought after, nor are the fruits of apostolic labor to be presumptuously expected from their use; but judgment as to their genuinity and proper use belongs to those who are appointed leaders in the Church, to whose special competence it belongs, not indeed to extinguish the Spirit, but to test all things and hold fast to that which is good.[20]

In chapter 4, *Lumen Gentium* presented the mission of the laity, framing it into a notion still tied to the traditional concept of "Catholic action in society":

Besides this apostolate which certainly pertains to all Christians, the laity can also be called in various ways to a more direct form of cooperation in the apostolate of the Hierarchy. This was the way certain men and women assisted Paul the Apostle in the Gospel, laboring much in the Lord. Further, they have the capacity to assume from the Hierarchy certain ecclesiastical functions, which are to be performed for a spiritual purpose.[21]

Through a rather ecclesiastical and not at all "movementist" view of the history of early Christianity as presented in the New Testament, *Lumen Gentium* described the role of the laity as strictly tied to the hierarchy both for its aim and its form: that is, as a complement to the role of the ecclesiastical hierarchy. Vatican II never addressed the fundamental issue of the institutional and canonical setting of the organized laity. Nor did the Council debate the issue of the canonical and theological consequences of the "ecclesiology of the people of God," that is, a new ordering of the relationship between hierarchy and clergy on one side and the hierarchy and organized laity on the other. The established subjection of Catholic Action to the hierarchy, as Pius XI and Pius XII had institutionalized it, remained the backdrop of the debate on the laity that took place at Vatican II. The debate on the organizations of the laity never took place because the juridical aspects of the Church of Vatican II were deferred to the new Code of Canon Law (promulgated by John Paul II only in 1983), which served during the Council as an excuse for the Roman Curia to postpone debate on the juridical consequences of the ecclesiology of Vatican II.[22]

The letter of *Gaudium et Spes* recalled the concept of "animation of temporal realities," although it did not make any progress in exploring the responsibilities of the organizations of lay Catholics toward the Church and the modern world:

> Secular duties and activities belong properly although not exclusively to laymen. Therefore acting as citizens in the world, whether individually or socially, they will keep the laws proper to each discipline, and labor to equip themselves with a genuine expertise in their various fields. They will gladly work with men seeking the same goals. Acknowledging the demands of faith and endowed with its force, they will unhesitatingly devise new enterprises, where they are appropriate, and put them into action. Laymen should also know that it is generally the function of their well-formed Christian conscience to see that the divine law is inscribed in the life of the earthly city; from priests they may look for spiritual light and nourishment.[23]

This was the classical division of duties between laymen and women on one side and clergy on the other. If we consider the situation inside the post–Vatican II Catholic movements, roles of the laity and clergy have intertwined in a way that makes it difficult to return to the letter of the Council documents. It is well known that in the mainstream of the new movements, the laity has taken on duties traditionally belonging to the clergy (preaching, teaching theology, relationship with the bishops and the Roman Curia). It is fair to say that the Council documents prepared the ground for the post–Vatican II movements, but also that the post–Vatican II movements can and do find a rationale in Vatican II or post–Vatican II "spirit" far more than in its documents.[24]

It is to be noted that the documents of Vatican II about the laity remained firmly within the pre–Vatican II theology of the laity, according to which the laity was supposed to back and cooperate with the hierarchy, with very little leeway for the laity to have a leading role in the Church. Therefore, a literal interpretation of these texts provides no room for the flourishing variety of new movements within the Catholic Church. This theology of the laity was also directed to a laity still integrated in local churches.

We must read Vatican II's documents on the lay apostolate in a framework of dualism between hierarchy and laity, which was overcome in the 1980s and 1990s through a silent yet epoch-making shift in Vatican policy toward the movements, that is, the support coming from John Paul II's plan for a "new evangelization" in Europe and in the Western world.[25]

In the Vatican II documents, we cannot find a description of how to organize the communion of laywomen and men: the faithful have a right to organize their apostolate as long as it is in communion with the hierarchy. *Apostolicam Actuositatem* 15–22 expressed, in theological language, "mobilization" as a key element of twentieth-century Western sociopolitical history, but it was a mobilization under the control of the ecclesiastical hierarchy. In the history of the Catholic Church between Pius XI and Pius XII, especially in Europe, Catholic Action worked as both the engine and brakes for lay commitment in the Church and in society. The "letter" of Vatican II confirmed both the institutional framework and ecclesial centrality of Catholic Action for the future of the Church. But the "spirit," it is argued, was in accord with the development of the movements.

The "letter" of Vatican II, therefore, was based on a different perspective from the one pursued by the new movements. On the one hand, the Council documents affirmed the importance of the lay organizations, trying to tie them to Catholic Action. On the other, the variety of lay organizations somehow recognized by Vatican II should be inserted into its ecclesiology, an ecclesiology of ressourcement, with an emphasis on the bishop and the local church, and on the proclaimed need for a more *ressourced* and thus "participatory" Church (parish councils, diocesan councils).[26]

If the "letter" of the documents of Vatican II endorses the movements, it is mostly *e silentio*—because of what it does *not* say. The real endorsement came from "the spirit" of the post–Vatican II Church. The post–Vatican II biographical and theological path of Cardinal Suenens illustrates the complexity of the relationship between the Vatican II drive for reform and the flourishing of the Catholic movements. A few years after being one of the most active and vocal advocates of reform and collegiality in the Church, on the floor of St. Peter during the Council and immediately afterward, he gave a major endorsement to the Catholic Charismatic Renewal.[27]

FROM VATICAN II TO THE NEW ECCLESIAL MOVEMENTS

Even though the new Catholic movements, their leaders, and the profound reasons supporting these movements were completely absent from the floor of the Council and from the texts debated and approved between 1960 and 1965, Vatican II represents, in the official biography of the new Catholic movements, a crucial moment: the movements' "birth certificate," evidence of their orthodoxy, and shield from every possible criticism against them.

This link between Vatican II and the movements may be theologically acceptable, but it is questionable from a historical point of view. On one hand, the metamorphosis of the organized Catholic laity started between World War II and Vatican II through a dissemination of new and different groups created by leaders coming from Catholic Action. This dissemination gave the new groups some inspiration taken from the reform movements of the late nineteenth and early twentieth century (but without the emphasis on reform as their outcome, and without the scholarly and intellectual work that marked the biblical, liturgical, patristic, and ecumenical movements). It grew from the need to reorganize the Catholic laity on a more participative (if not "democratic") basis and as an outreach beyond the cultural boundaries of Tridentine Catholicism. The Catholic sociology of the *pastorale d'ensemble* and new way of clustering Catholic Action into new associations gathering the Catholic laity along generational and professional lines were two sides of the same "updating" of the laity in European Catholicism.[28]

On the other hand, the real flourishing of the new Catholic movements started only after Vatican II and through an implicit denial of some basic markers of the brief season of the earlier Catholic Action, even as it was understood at Vatican II. A first decisive element in this transition was the change of paradigm in Catholic ecclesiology.[29] Post–Vatican II policy, with its emphasis on the laity, made the classical distinction between the *duo genera christianorum*—clergy and laity, clearly separated—look old. It also upset Vatican II's carefully worded description of the balance of power within the Church between pope and bishops. The new Catholic movements took that window of opportunity to protect their own community ecclesiology, thus neglecting the local dimension of the communion of the Church and choosing the universal Church and its symbol—the pope, as the first and last controller of their catholicity—just as the mendicant orders did in the Middle Ages.[30] In that process, the movements were one of the winners of the post–Vatican II power struggle in the Catholic Church, whose results were the undermining of the bishops' authority and the despair of the "unorganized laity" in some local churches.

A second factor, linked to the new ecclesiology, was the crisis of Catholic Action, of its identity and membership, as the unique container of the enthusiasm of the Catholic laity. As the Catholic Church opened itself to the world, Catholic Action lost a great deal of its original mission to educate the faithful and preserve the Catholic laity from the attacks coming from the liberal ideologies and totalitarian regimes in Europe. In a politically and socially less hostile environment, moreover, the end of the political and social Catholic ghetto meant that Catholic Action was not as needed as it was before World War II.

Far from being an organized plot to take over the Church, every single movement after Vatican II walked its own way according to its own Catholic identity, theological options, and cultural background. The pattern was not a common ideology, theology, or spirituality, but a common struggle to survive in an ecclesiastically hostile environment. The movements that survived the decade after Vatican II had faced the difficulty of obtaining recognition of their existence within the Catholic communion from the Church institution. That period produced the scars of the untold suffering of the new Catholic movements, which soon turned their early experience of the Church's lack of understanding of their religious experience into self-promotion within the ranks of John Paul II's Church.[31]

From the beginning of John Paul II's pontificate, the new Catholic movements experienced success and endorsement by the official teaching of the Church and especially by the pope himself.[32] Organizations and movements such as Opus Dei, Focolare, Neocatecumenal Way, and the Catholic Charismatic Renewal managed to make themselves trustworthy, mostly by putting the greatest possible distance between themselves and the "Catholic dissent" fringe movements, and by choosing loyalty to the Holy See and to the pope as their ultimate virtue. They sometimes did this at the cost of making enemies of the national bishops' conferences or of the bishops in whose dioceses they were active.[33] In any case, the success or failure of a new movement depended greatly on its ability to connect with the top of the ecclesiastical institution and that institution's theological agenda regarding the global Church.

THE NEW CATHOLIC MOVEMENTS AND THE CENTER-PERIPHERY ISSUE

The spectacular rise of the movements has continued and yet has been rife with problems and inner tensions with the Church and among the movements themselves.[34] The phenomenon of the new movements has in any case much more to do with post–Vatican II than with the Council as such: "One of the most striking developments in Catholic life since the council ended has been the flourishing of 'movements' such as Opus Dei, the Neo-Catechumenate, Communion and Liberation, and so on."[35] But the movements' claim of the legacy of Vatican II raises the issue of the reception of Vatican II and especially of the reception of the core message of the Council, that is, the main issues of the most important event in the history of modern Catholicism.[36]

In the conclusions to his book, John O'Malley emphasizes the three "issues under the issues" of the Council: (1) Vatican II as a *language-event*; (2) the possibility of *change* in the Church; and (3) the *relationship between center and periphery*.[37] The importance of these three issues appears even more important if we try to understand the relations between the Council and one of the most spectacular phenomena of post–Vatican II, such as the new Catholic movements. The most important among these issues, in order to understand the importance of the relationship between the new Catholic movements and Vatican II, is the relationship between center and periphery.

In his conclusions, John O'Malley emphasizes the importance of the center-periphery issue and its relationship to collegiality, making the case for the link between ecclesiology, ressourcement, and the new role of the bishops in Vatican II Catholicism.[38] From that point of view, the history of the post–Vatican II Catholic movements proves problematic, given the fact that the dramatic crisis of the bishops' authority in the Church and the flourishing of the movements is more than a coincidence.

According to Nicholas Lash, "there are, at present, few more urgent tasks facing the Church than that of realizing the as-yet unrealized program of Vatican II by throwing into reverse the centralization of power which accrued during the twentieth century, and restoring episcopal authority to the episcopate."[39] It is a fact that the new movements tend to describe themselves as the twentieth-century equivalent of the mendicant orders in the Middle Ages or the Jesuits in the Tridentine era. Even if it were true, such an attempt to explain their flourishing in the Catholic Church proves the ecclesiological inclinations of the new movements. Despite the differences between the movements' ecclesiologies (for example, between Opus Dei and the Catholic Charismatic Renewal), their success comes at the expense of the ecclesiology of the local church, thus helping to undermine the quest for a new balance between center and periphery in modern-world Catholicism.

Although some of the new Catholic movements have received and enriched the modernity of the Church and have taken to heart some important issues of the social teaching of the Church, so far their development and growth within the Catholic Church has been largely marked by scant awareness of the relationship between collegiality and the bishops' role and by a non-synodal model of governance with their communities (if we look at the role of the leaders and the founders in some of the most successful movements).[40]

The success of the movements, in that regard, proves the failure, or at least the difficulty of the ecclesiology of the local church between the end of the twentieth century and the beginning of the twenty-first century.[41] The direct appeal to the papacy and the bypassing of the local bishops were justified in past centuries by the "threats" of Conciliarism in the fifteenth century and by the moral corruption of noble bishops in sixteenth-century European Catholicism.[42] But in Vatican II Catholicism, such an ecclesial praxis is hardly justifiable from an ecclesiological point of view.[43] The rejection of the ecclesiology of the local church (*communion*) in favor of an ecclesiology of the group (*community*) means not only a rejection of the *ressourcement* ecclesiology of Vatican II, but also a substantial refusal to acknowledge the center-periphery issue.[44]

The epoch-making shift made possible by Vatican II from a hierarchical, institutional ecclesiology to one centered on *communio* implies a new pattern of relationship among pope, bishops, clergy, and laity, and between Rome and the local churches. At the local level, the new ecclesiology of Vatican II means not only the resurgence of synods, provincial councils and plenary councils, the need for which had been ignored for four centuries, but also the actual putting into operation of the new councils and boards created by Vatican II at the diocesan and parish level.[45]

In the intention of Vatican II, these new institutions were supposed to redress the balance of power within the local church, stressing the ordinary powers of bishops alongside the pope's extraordinary powers in the government of dioceses and enabling the participation of laity in the life of local churches, not just through liturgy and social action, but also by taking part in the theological reception of Vatican II.[46] In the last three decades, the practical ecclesiology of the movements has facilitated the end of the bishop- and clergy-led local church. But this step has not been in the direction of a more participatory local church, as is clear from the problematic relationship between the movements on one side and the parish pastoral council, the diocesan pastoral councils, and the diocesan synods on the other.[47] From this point of view, if we can define *synodality* as the capability of the Church to hear every member of the faithful's voice—through liturgy, through parish experience, through participation in the visible Church structures such as pastoral councils and diocesan synods— the contribution of the new Catholic movements has been multifaceted and diverse, but often presenting a "ticket mentality" typical of a "closed-community Catholicism" more than the syn-odal face of "church as communion." The movements have replaced the participatory model with a more leader-driven model of Christian community, where inner diversity is paradoxically far less present and less welcome than in the past.[48]

Of course we can identify important differences between the movements, and it is possible to divide the movements with respect to their model of governance: revanche-driven movements with a strong antiliberal political and religious culture (Opus Dei, Communion and Liberation, Legionaries of Christ, Neocatechu-menal Way); more open Pentecostal-Charismatic movements (Charismatic Renewal, Cursillos, Focolare); Catholic elites active in the neomonastic communities or movements close to the res-sourcement and the ecumenical rapprochement (Communities of Sant'Egidio).[49] But sometimes a neo-universalist ecclesiology, which is at the core of some of the new movements' identity and ecclesial praxis, acts as an undeclared disowning of Vatican II col-legiality, and goes far beyond Vatican I–style infallibility.[50] Their political option for an ecclesiology based almost exclusively on obedience to the pope, applied through an intense communitari-anism that almost completely bypasses communion with the local churches (their bishops and parishes), has heavy implications for the issue of freedom in the Church. The twentieth-century struggle to rediscover the ancient, patristic conciliar and synodal tradition in the Church seems to have had a short life. The post–Vatican II, antimodern anguish embodied by the movements has contributed to the present difficulty of the conciliar and synodal institutions in the church and to the reduction of subsidiarity in the relations between Rome and the local churches.[51]

From this point of view, the success of the movements in the church of John Paul II is directly proportional to the capability of some of those movements to undermine the call for a more synodal and less centralized Church. If it is true that Vatican II pushed for a new balance between center and periphery in the Church through a new discovery of collegiality thanks to "a process of *ressource-ment*,"[52] then the practical ecclesiology of many of the new Catholic movements has been leaning toward a modern or postmodern model of one-man infallible leadership, much more than toward a first-millennium, ressourcement ecclesiology of collegiality.

The post–Vatican II history of the reform of ecclesiastical institutions has shown that the Council affirmations on collegiality did not touch the shape and form of the power of the Bishop of Rome. From a church politics point of view, the difficult implementation of collegiality in the seventies left the new movements untouched. The movements played a role, especially from the 1980s on, in giving the Catholic Church a new face that cheerfully complied with the doctrinal policy of John Paul II. From an ecclesiological point of view, the shortcomings of Vatican II ecclesiology of the local church received serious blows when some of the most media-savvy movements (such as Opus Dei, Communion and Liberation, and Neocatechumenal Way) deliberately bypassed the authority of the local bishops and sought protection directly from the Holy See, whose doctrinal focus (on issues like moral theology and theology of liberation) was much more in harmony with the movements than with the bishops and the national bishops' conferences at that time.[53] As unpopular as some bishops might be (especially in some countries), this takeover of the collegial voice of the bishops and national conferences has hardly improved the relationship between center and periphery in the post–Vatican II Catholic Church.

The movements' church politics has reduced the already very limited breathing room for collegiality in the post–Vatican II period, not differently from the role played by some new religious orders together with the Roman Curia in undermining the role of the bishops that was restored and reformed at Trent.[54] But the main difference between the post-Trent religious orders and the post–Vatican II movements is their contribution to the culture of Catholicism. The new Catholic movements defined themselves or were defined as the fruit of Vatican II because of their support of John Paul II's style of enforcing the Council, despite their scant contribution to the theological debate in the post–Vatican II Church.

DISCERNING THE SPIRITS OF VATICAN II: CONCLUSIONS

From a first analysis of the mainstream movements' reception of the Council's "issues under the issues," the complexity of the relationship between the movements and Vatican II is clear. The movements have absorbed Vatican II not in the literal meaning of its final documents, but they have appealed to its "spirit," being repeatedly encouraged to do so by John Paul II's teaching and doctrinal policy toward them. It is time to go beyond the "mythical history" of the relationship between Vatican II and the new Catholic movements: the ecclesial movements' need for foundational myths does not excuse Church historians from doing their job. Historical evidence tells us that the movements as such had no role among the participants at Vatican II or in the final documents of the Council. In fact, from the 1980s on, they turned to the often repudiated "spirit of Vatican II," since they had little opportunity to find support in conciliar texts themselves.[55]

In this critical moment of the reception of Vatican II, at fifty years from its conclusion, the issue of the "spirit of the Council" is more important than ever. German ecclesiologist Hermann Pottmeyer called for a discernment of spirits already in the 1980s:

> The reception of the Council as a movement is an equally unfinished business. This aspect of the Council is sometimes referred to as its "spirit"; what is meant is the intellectual and spiritual impulse toward renewal that animated the work of the Council itself and that emanates from it. "Spirit" is also a theologically appropriate description....Here the task confronting a hermeneutic of the Council goes far beyond an objective interpretation of the texts. Something more is needed: a *discretio spirituum*, a recognition and distinction or discernment of spirits.[56]

More recently, and with a historically more secure awareness of "what happened at Vatican II," John O'Malley has addressed the issue of the spirit of the Council:

> For the first time in history, a council would take care self-consciously to infuse its documents with vocabulary and themes that cut across them all. In that sense Vatican II conveyed a "spirit."...In revealing the spirit it

reveals not a momentary effervescence but a consistent and verifiable reorientation.[57]

This general reorientation was articulated in a characteristic vocabulary and a "style of Church," and originated from the set of new urgencies, sensibilities, and proposals generated by the meeting of the universal episcopate.[58] In this reorientation, the center-periphery issue was crucial: "The centralized 'implementation'... that had followed the Council of Trent belonged to a type of council and a cultural stage now completely of the past."[59]

For that reason, it is time to reframe the debate on Vatican II and its spirit and try to "discern the spirits" of Vatican II in relation to some new form of Western Catholicism, such as the movements. While some elements of their reception of Vatican II are susceptible to being presented as reception of the Council teaching (new centrality of the laity in the groups' and communities' spiritual leadership, engagement in public-policy issues, biblical and patristic renewal in their cultural identity), other elements seem far more problematic if we consider both the documents and the debate at Vatican II (universalist ecclesiology and disregard of the authority of the local bishops; antisynodal attitude; "ticket mentality" in their relationship toward the modern world). Their reception of the Council seems much more like a trajectory than something already accomplished.

In the past three decades, the term *spirit of Vatican II* has been used in the Catholic Church in different ways and has received different assessments. Some interpreters of that spirit, such as the movements, have been praised by leading figures in the hierarchy for embodying a creative way of being faithful to the "real" spirit of Vatican II, whereas theologians and historians have been harshly criticized for even using the expression. Especially during the pontificates of John Paul II and Benedict XVI, a double standard was applied, as if the spirit of Vatican II is good for the movements but bad when used by professional historians and theologians in their quest for a consistent hermeneutics for the Council.[60]

Nonetheless, it should be clear by now that the attempt to ban "the spirit of Vatican II" from the language of historical and theological debate on the Council is hazardous, unproductive, inconsistent, and above all, unfaithful to the reality of the Council. When the spirit is rightly understood as expressing basic orientations of the Council that, while based on the documents, cut across most all of them, it is indispensable for understanding and interpreting the Council. In this sense, the history of the new ecclesial movements and of their reception of Vatican II is paradigmatic of some key dynamics in the reception of Vatican II by the whole Church.[61]

Notes

1. See Charles Whitehead, "The Role of Ecclesial Movements and New Communities in the Life of the Church," in *New Religious Movements in the Catholic Church*, ed. Michael A. Hayes (New York: Burns & Oates, 2005), 18.

2. For the polemics about the "spirit of Vatican II," see Cardinal Camillo Ruini (vicar for the diocese of Rome), in Rome, June 17, 2005, presenting Agostino Marchetto's *Il concilio ecumenico Vaticano II. Contrappunto per la sua storia* (Vatican City: Libreria Editrice Vaticana, 2005), private audio recording. From Card. Ruini, see also the introduction to Karol Wojtyla, *Alle fonti del rinnovamento. Studio sull'attuazione del Concilio Vaticano II*, foreword by Card. Camillo Ruini (Soveria Mannelli: Rubbettino, 2007), v–ix. Similar opinions are evident in Matthew L. Lamb and Matthew Levering, "Introduction," in *Vatican II: Renewal within Tradition*, ed. Matthew L. Lamb and Matthew Levering (New York: Oxford University Press, 2008), 4–7. On the other side, see Alberto Melloni, "Concili, ecumenicità e storia. Note di discussion," *Cristianesimo nella Storia* 28 (2007): 509–42. About the history of the debate on Vatican II, see Massimo Faggioli, *Vatican II: The Battle for Meaning* (Mahwah, NJ: Paulist Press, 2012).

3. See John W. O'Malley, *What Happened at Vatican II* (Cambridge, MA: Belknap Press of Harvard University Press, 2008), 304.

4. See ibid., 53–92.

5. See Émile Poulat, *Histoire, dogme et critique dans la crise moderniste* (Paris: Casterman, 1962, 1979).

6. For the pre–Vatican II reform movements, see Étienne Fouilloux, "I movimenti di riforma nel pensiero cattolica del XIX e XX secolo," in *I movimenti nella storia del cristianesimo. Caratteristiche, variazioni, continuità (Cristianesimo nella Storia 34/2003)*, ed. Giuseppe Alberigo and Massimo Faggioli, 659–76. About the movements before and after Vatican II in the United States, see James M. O'Toole, *The Faithful: A History of Catholics*

in America (Cambridge, MA: Belknap Press of Harvard University Press, 2008), esp. 144–265.

7. See François Laplanche, *La crise de l'origine: la science catholique des Évangiles et l'histoire au XXe siècle* (Paris: Albin Michel, 2006); Bernard Montagnes, *Père Lagrange, 1855–1938. The Story of Father Marie-Joseph Lagrange: Founder of Modern Catholic Bible Study* (New York: Paulist Press, 2006).

8. See Annibale Bugnini, *The Reform of the Liturgy, 1948–1975* (Collegeville, MN: Liturgical, 1990); Keith F. Pecklers, *The Unread Vision: The Liturgical Movement in the United States of America, 1926–1955* (Collegeville, MN: Liturgical, 1998); Maria Paiano, *Liturgia e società nel Novecento. Percorsi del movimento liturgico di fronte ai processi di secolarizzazione* (Rome: Edizioni di Storia e Letteratura, 2000); Raymond Loonbeek and Jacques Mortiau, *Un pionnier, Dom Lambert Beauduin (1873–1960). Liturgie et unité des chrétiens* (Louvain-la-Neuve: Collège Erasme, 2001); Andrea Grillo, *La nascita della liturgia nel XX secolo. Saggio sul rapporto tra movimento liturgico e (post-) modernità* (Assisi: Cittadella, 2003); Massimo Faggioli, *True Reform: Liturgy and Ecclesiology in "Sacrosanctum Concilium"* (Collegeville, MN: Liturgical, 2012).

9. See Yves Congar, *Chrétiens désunis. Principes d'un "œcuménisme" catholique* (Paris: Cerf, 1937); Étienne Fouilloux, *Les catholiques et l'unité chrétienne du XIXe au XXe siècle: itinéraires européens d'expression française* (Paris: Centurion, 1982); Mauro Velati, *Una difficile transizione. Il cattolicesimo tra unionismo ed ecumenismo (1952–1964)* (Bologna: Il Mulino, 1996).

10. See Étienne Fouilloux, *La Collection "Sources chrétiennes." Éditer les Pères de l'Église au XXe siècle* (Paris: Cerf, 1995).

11. See Joseph Ratzinger, *I movimenti ecclesiali e la loro collocazione teologica*, in Pontificium Consilium pro Laicis, *I movimenti nella Chiesa: atti del Congresso mondiale dei movimenti ecclesiali* (Rome, May 27–29, 1998) (Vatican City: Libreria Editrice Vaticana, 1999), 23–51 (in English: *Movements in the Church: Proceedings of the World Congress of the Ecclesial Movements*, Rome, 27–29 May 1998 [Vatican City: Pontificium Consilium pro Laicis, 1999]); John Paul II, homily at the Mass of Pentecost with the Catholic Movements (Rome, May 31, 2000); Joseph Cardinal Ratzinger (Pope Benedict XVI), *New Outpourings of the Spirit: Movements in the Church* (San Francisco: Ignatius, 2007). See also the address of the secretary of the Pontifical Council for the Laity at the International conference for the bishops organized by the Pontifical Council (Rocca di Papa, May 15–17, 2008), Joseph Clemens, "Papa Ratzinger e i movimenti," *Il Regno-documenti* 13 (2008): 441–49; Pontificium Consilium

pro Laicis, *The Beauty of Being a Christian: Movements in the Church* (Vatican City: Libreria Editrice Vaticana, 2007).

12. The movements "represent one of the most significant fruits of that springtime in the Church which was foretold by the Second Vatican Council": John Paul II, *Message*, May 27, 1998, in Pontificium Consilium pro Laicis, *Movements in the Church. Proceedings of the World Congress of the Ecclesial Movements* (Vatican City: Libreria Editrice Vaticana, 1999), 16.

13. See Liliana Ferrari, *Una storia dell'Azione cattolica. Gli ordinamenti statutari da Pio XI a Pio XII* (Genoa: Marietti, 1989); Angelica Steinmaus-Pollak, *Das als katholische Aktion organisierte Laienapostolat: Geschichte seiner Theorie und seiner kirchenrechtlichen Praxis in Deutschland* (Würzburg: Echter, 1988); Leo R. Ward, *Catholic Life, U.S.A. Contemporary Lay Movements* (St. Louis: Herder, 1959); David O'Brien, *Public Catholicism* (New York: Macmillan, 1989).

14. See O'Malley, *What Happened at Vatican II*, 229–30, and O'Toole, *The Faithful*, 145–98.

15. See especially Yves Congar, *Lay People in the Church: A Study for a Theology of the Laity* (Westminster, MD: Newman Press, 1957).

16. Opus Dei (a rather particular movement marked by a high degree of clericalization) was created in 1928, but most of the other Catholic movements were founded between the end of World War II and the 1970s. In this sense, Opus Dei and Legionaries of Christ rose from a similar culture and in the same period in the history of the new ecclesial movements.

17. See Barbara Zadra, *I movimenti ecclesiali e i loro statuti* (Rome: Pontificia Università Gregoriana, 1997); Velasio De Paolis, "Diritto dei fedeli di associarsi e la normativa che lo regola," in *Fedeli Associazioni Movimenti* (Milan: Glossa, 2002) 127–62.

18. See *History of Vatican II*, ed. Giuseppe Alberigo, English version ed. Joseph A. Komonchak, esp. vol. 4, *Church as Communion. Third Period and Intersession. September 1964–September 1965* (Maryknoll, NY: Orbis, 2004); Zadra, *I movimenti ecclesiali e i loro statuti*, 7–21.

19. Vatican II, decree *Apostolicam Actuositatem*, paragraph 20. Those four criteria—apostolic aim, cooperation with the hierarchy, unity of the laity, and mandate of the hierarchy—would be subsequently developed by John Paul II's apostolic exhortation *Christifideles Laici* (1988). See Guido Bausenhart, "Theologischer Kommentar zum Dekret über das Apostolat des Laien," in *Herders Theologischer Kommentar zum Zweiten Vatikanischen Konzil*, ed. Hans Jochen Hilberath and Peter Hünermann, vol. 4 (Freiburg i.B.: Herder, 2005), 5–123.

20. Vatican II, constitution *Lumen Gentium*, paragraph 12.

21. Ibid., paragraph 33. See Gérard Philips, *La Chiesa e il suo mistero nel Concilio Vaticano II: storia, testo e commento della Costituzione Lumen Gentium*, vol. 2 (Milan: Jaca Book, 1969), 30–62 (or *L'Église et son mystère au IIe Concile du Vatican. Histoire, text et commentaire de la constitution "Lumen gentium"* [Paris-Tournai, Desclée, 1967]); Peter Hünermann, "Theologischer Kommentar zur dogmatischen Konstitution über die Kirche," in *Herders Theologischer Kommentar zum Zweiten Vatikanischen Konzil*, ed. Hans Jochen Hilberath and Peter Hünermann, vol. 2 (Freiburg i.B.: Herder, 2004), 263–582, esp. 468–71; Ciro García Fernández, "De la 'teología de los laicos' de Lumen gentium a los 'movimientos eclesiales' posconciliares," *Burgense* 48, no. 1 (2007): 45–82.

22. The 1983 Code of Canon Law addressed the issue of the organizations of the laity, even if in a way that did not please the supporters of the new lay apostolate: see Eugenio Corecco, "Aspects of the Reception of Vatican II in the Code of Canon Law," in *The Reception of Vatican II*, ed. Giuseppe Alberigo, Jean-Pierre Jossua, and Joseph A. Komonchak (Washington, DC: The Catholic University of America Press, 1987), 249–96.

23. Vatican II, constitution *Gaudium et Spes*, paragraph 43. For the history of the constitution, see Giovanni Turbanti, *Un concilio per il mondo moderno: la redazione della costituzione pastorale "Gaudium et spes" del Vaticano II* (Bologna: Il Mulino, 2000); Norman P. Tanner, *The Church and the World: Gaudium et Spes, Inter Mirifica* (Mahwah, NJ: Paulist Press, 2005).

24. See Franco Giulio Brambilla, "Le aggregazioni ecclesiali nei documenti del magistero dal concilio fino ad oggi," *La Scuola Cattolica* 116 (1988): 461–511.

25. See Bruno Forte, "Associazioni, movimenti e missione nella chiesa locale," *Il Regno-documenti* 1 (1983): 29–34; Juan José Etxeberría, "Los movimentos eclesiales en los albores del siglo XXI," *Revista Española de Derecho Canonico* 58 (2001): 577–616.

26. See Fernand Boulard, "La curie et les conseils diocésains," in *La charge pastorale des évêques. Texte, traduction et commentaires* (Paris: Cerf, 1969), 241–74; Georg Kretschmar, *Das bischöfliche Amt. Kirchengeschichtliche und ökumenische Studien zur Frage des kirchlichen Amtes*, ed. Dorothea Wendebourg (Göttingen: Vandenhoeck & Ruprecht, 1999); Massimo Faggioli, *Il vescovo e il concilio. Modello episcopale e aggiornamento al Vaticano II* (Bologna: Il Mulino, 2005); Massimo Faggioli, "Institutions of Episcopal Synodality-Collegiality after Vatican II: The Decree *Christus Dominus* and the Agenda for Synodality-Collegiality in the 21st Century," *The Jurist* 64, no. 2 (2004): 224–46.

27. See Leon-Joseph Suenens, *A New Pentecost?* (London: Darton Longman & Todd, 1974); Leon-Joseph Suenens, *Memories and Hopes* (Dublin: Veritas, 1992).

28. See Joseph Debès, Émile Poulat, *L'appel de la JOC. 1926–1928* (Paris: Cerf, 1986); Françoise Richou, *La Jeunesse ouvrière chrétienne (JOC). Genèse d'une jeunesse militante* (Paris: L'Harmattan, 1997).

29. See Richard P. McBrien, *The Church: The Evolution of Catholicism* (New York: Harper, 2008), 182–92; about the new movements 345–49.

30. See Giovanni Miccoli, *Chiesa gregoriana: ricerche sulla riforma del secolo XI* (Rome: Edizioni di Storia e Letteratura, 1999), 1–58.

31. On the support experienced during John Paul II's pontificate by Opus Dei, Legion of Christ, Communion and Liberation, The Neocatechumenate, Focolare, and the Community of Sant'Egidio, see McBrien, *The Church*, 345–47. On the movements and the government of Church under John Paul II, see Thomas J. Reese, *Inside the Vatican: The Politics and Organization of the Catholic Church* (Cambridge, MA: Harvard University Press, 1998); Daniele Hervieu-Lèger, "Le croyant et l'institution," in *Le gouvernement de l'église catholique. Synodes et exercice du pouvoir*, ed. Jacques Palard (Paris: Cerf, 1997), 313–22.

32. See Giancarlo Rocca, *L'Opus Dei. Appunti e documenti per una storia* (Milan: Paoline, 1985); Enzo Maria Fondi, Michele Zanzucchi, *Un popolo nato dal Vangelo. Chiara Lubich e i Focolari* (Cinisello B.: San Paolo, 2003); Bernhard Sven Anuth, *Der Neokatechumenale Weg: Geschichte, Erscheinungsbild, Rechtscharakter* (Würzburg: Echter, 2006); Jean Duchesne, *"Jesus Revolution" Made in U.S.A.* (Paris: Cerf, 1972); Salvatore Abbruzzese, *Comunione e Liberazione. Identité catholique et disqualification du monde* (Paris, Cerf: 1989); Peter Zimmerling, *Die charismatischen Bewegungen. Theologie—Spiritualität—Anstöße zum Gespräch* (Göttingen: Vandenhoeck & Ruprecht, 2001); Andrea Riccardi, *Sant'Egidio, Rome et le monde. Entretiens avec Jean-Dominique Durand et Regis Ladous* (Paris: Beauchesne, 1996).

33. For case of Italy, see Massimo Faggioli, "Tra referendum sul divorzio e revisione del Concordato. Enrico Bartoletti segretario della CEI (1972–1976)," *Contemporanea* 2 (2001): 255–80.

34. See, for example, Massimo Faggioli, "1968 and the New Elite of Italian Catholicism," in *Catholic Historical Review* 98, no. 1 (January 2012): 18–40.

35. Nicholas Lash, *Theology for Pilgrims* (Notre Dame: University of Notre Dame Press, 2008), 236.

36. See, for example, Gianfranco Calabrese, "Quaestiones Disputatae: Chiesa come 'popolo di Dio' o Chiesa come 'comunione'? Ermeneutica e recezione della Lumen Gentium," *Rassegna di teologia* 5 (2005): 695–718; Gilles Routhier, "A 40 anni dal concilio Vaticano II. Un lungo tirocinio verso un nuovo tipo di cattolicesimo," *La Scuola Cattolica* 133 (2005): 19–51.

37. See O'Malley, *What Happened at Vatican II*, 298–313.

38. See ibid., 302–5.

39. Lash, *Theology for Pilgrims*, 234.

40. See Marvin L. Krier Mich, *Catholic Social Teaching and Movements* (Mystic, CT: Twenty-Third Publications, 1998); Alessandro Rovello, *La morale e i movimenti ecclesiali* (Bologna: EDB, 2013).

41. See Joseph Ratzinger, "L'ecclesiologia della Costituzione Lumen Gentium," in *Il Concilio Vaticano II. Recezione e attualità alla luce del Giubileo*, ed. Rino Fisichella (Cinisello B.: San Paolo, 2000), 66–81; Walter Kasper, "Das Verhältnis von Universalkirche und Ortskirche. Freundschaftliche Auseinandersetzung mit der Kritik von Joseph Kardinal Ratzinger," *Stimmen der Zeit* 12 (2000): 795–804; Hervé-Marie Legrand, "Les évêques, les églises locales et l'église entière. Évolutions institutionelles depuis Vatican II et chantiers actuels de recherche," *Revue de Sciences philosophiques et théologiques* 85 (2001): 461–509.

42. See Klaus Ganzer, "Gesamtkirche und Ortskirche auf dem Konzil von Trient," *Römische Quartalschrift* 95, nos. 3–4 (2000): 167–78; Massimo Faggioli, "Chiese locali ed ecclesiologia prima e dopo il concilio di Trento," in *Storia della Chiesa in Europa tra ordinamento politico-amministrativo e strutture ecclesiastiche*, ed. Luciano Vaccaro (Brescia: Morcelliana, 2005), 197–213.

43. See, for example, the case involving the local bishops and the Redemptoris Mater Seminary that the Neocatechumenal Way runs in Japan: see Massimo Faggioli, "The Neocatechumenate and Communion in the Church," *Japan Mission Journal* 65, no. 1 (Spring 2011): 46–53.

44. See Jean-Marie R. Tillard, *L'église locale: ecclésiologie de communion et catholicité*, (Paris: Cerf, 1995), 250–71 and 397–410.

45. For some examples of the everlasting life of the idea of a synodal Church, see *Synod and Synodality: Theology, History, Canon Law and Ecumenism in New Contact*, ed. Alberto Melloni and Silvia Scatena (Münster: LIT, 2005).

46. See Massimo Faggioli, *A Council for the Global Church: Receiving Vatican II in History* (Minneapolis, MN: Fortress Press, 2015).

47. See Jacques Palard, "L'istitution catholique en recherches. L'acteur, le théologien et le sociologue," in *Le gouvernement de l'église catholique*, 7–57; Ghislain Lafont, *Imaginer l'église catholique* (Paris: Cerf, 1995; English translation, *Imagining the Catholic Church: Structured Communion in the Spirit* (Collegeville, MN: Liturgical, 2000).

48. For the "ticket mentality" in small community life, see Theodor W. Adorno et al., *The Authoritarian Personality* (New York: Harper, 1950).

49. For some tentative classifications of the new Catholic movements, see Faggioli, *Breve storia dei movimenti cattolici*, 119–20; Alberto

Melloni, "Movimenti. De significatione verborum" *Concilium* 3 (2003), *I movimenti nella chiesa*, ed. Alberto Melloni, 13–34; Daniele Hervieu-Léger, *Le pèlerin et le converti. La religion en movement* (Paris: Flammarion, 1999); Agostino Favale, *Movimenti ecclesiali contemporanei. Dimensioni storiche, teologico-spirituali ed apostoliche* (Rome: LAS: 1982 [vol. 2], 1991 [vol. 4]); Piersandro Vanzan, "Elementi comuni e identificativi dell'attuale fenomeno movimentista intraecclesiale con cenni a rischi e speranze," in *Fedeli Associazioni Movimenti* (Milan: Glossa, 2002), 187–206.

50. See Hermann J. Pottmeyer, *Towards a Papacy in Communion: Perspectives from Vatican Councils I & II* (New York: Crossroad, 1998); John R. Quinn, *The Reform of the Papacy* (New York: Herder & Herder, 2000).

51. See Massimo Faggioli, "Prassi e norme relative alle conferenze episcopali tra concilio Vaticano II e post-concilio (1959–1998)," in *Synod and Synodality*, 265–96.

52. O'Malley, *What Happened at Vatican II*, 302–3.

53. See Gilles Routhier, "Beyond Collegiality: The Local Church Left Behind by the Second Vatican Council," in *The Catholic Theological Society of America, Proceedings of the Sixty-second Annual Convention, 2007*, ed. Jonathan Y. Tan, 1–15.

54. See Hubert Jedin, "Delegatus Sedis Apostolicae und bischöfliche Gewalt auf dem Konzil von Trient," in *Die Kirche und ihre Ämter und Stände. Festgabe Joseph Kardinal Frings* (Köln: Bachem, 1960), 462–75 (republished in Huber Jedin, *Kirche des Glaubens, Kirche der Geschichte*, vol. 2 [Freiburg i.B.: Herder, 1966], 414–28).

55. See Zadra, *I movimenti ecclesiali e i loro statuti*, 7–21; Komonchak, *History of Council Vatican II*, vol. 4.

56. Hermann J. Pottmeyer, "Interpretation of the Council," in *The Reception of Vatican II*, 27–43, esp. 41.

57. O'Malley, *What Happened at Vatican II*, 310.

58. See John W. O'Malley, "Trent and Vatican II: Two Styles of Church," in *From Trent to Vatican II: Historical and Theological Investigations*, ed. Raymond F. Bulman and Frederick J. Parrella (New York: Oxford University Press, 2006), 301–20.

59. See Giuseppe Alberigo, "The New Shape of the Council," in *History of Vatican II*, ed. Giuseppe Alberigo, English version ed. Joseph A. Komonchak, vol. 3 (Maryknoll, NY: Orbis, 2000), 505.

60. About this, see Massimo Faggioli, "Vatican II: The History and the 'Narratives,'" *Theological Studies* 73, no. 4 (December 2012): 749–67.

61. See Massimo Faggioli, *A Council for the Global Church: Receiving Vatican II in History* (Minneapolis: Fortress, 2015).

6

THE NEW CATHOLIC MOVEMENTS, VATICAN II, AND FREEDOM IN THE CATHOLIC CHURCH

THE GLOBALIZED, MEDIA-FRIENDLY Catholicism of the twenty-first century has inherited from the political and ideological culture of the twentieth century a certain pattern of activism and a new type of faithful who practice this activism. This activist faithful is particularly visible in the new Catholic movements such as Opus Dei, Legionaries of Christ, Communion and Liberation, Community of Sant'Egidio, and Focolare. These movements mentioned here represent just a small sample of the new ecclesial entities, a small but growing and significant part of contemporary global Catholicism.

They were highly regarded in Rome, especially during the pontificates of John Paul II and Benedict XVI, who saw them as the best possible response against the challenge of a world that is radically secularized and massively unchurched. The new Catholic movements are the post-Christendom face of Catholicism. For this reason, they play a key role in the European church, but they are quietly and rapidly being exported to other countries with

113

strong Catholic communities, gaining momentum particularly in the Americas. They were not created by John Paul II or by Vatican II, despite what some of their members claim in a bid to portray themselves as above criticism.[1] In this sense, they are from a chronological point of view much more postconciliar than conciliar: an element that should be considered by the critics of the postconciliar period in assessing the aftermath of Vatican II.

One of the most interesting phenomena regarding the new movements is the kind of lay and clerical leadership they created and by which they were created. The movements are producing within the Catholic Church a fairly specific type of *new elite*, formed from both clerics and laypeople, which has very little to do with the social and intellectual elites that led the Catholic Church in medieval and modern times. This new elite embodies a new kind of leadership that seems innovative compared with the traditional Catholic elite (bishops, clergy, religious orders, monks, lay intellectuals, and politicians), when it comes to shaping strong communities and creating networks for spiritual and material welfare.

Moreover, the new movements have an articulated yet basic, apophatic yet intelligible, version of Catholicism, which could represent an epoch-making shift in the living body of the Catholic Church as it comes to grips with the challenge of postsecular politics in the Western world. The way these movements live out and advocate their on-stage, all-absorbing, and enthusiastic Catholicism deeply affects both the theological image and the very life of the Catholic Church as a communion of freedom, distinctively inflecting the ecclesiology of Vatican II.

THE RISE OF THE NEW CATHOLIC MOVEMENTS

The history of the Catholic movements begins in the late nineteenth century, in the wake of the cultural struggle between the new national states (specifically Italy, Belgium, Germany, and France) and a Catholic Church increasingly—and traumatically—deprived of its social and political power.[2] With the encouragement of Leo XIII and Pius X, a network of Catholic leagues, banks, trade unions, and workers' unions was formed in opposition to the social and economic establishment of the new liberal states in an effort to counter both the Marxist appeal and the domination imposed by capitalism on the life of the working class. Since Catholic political engagement was largely confined to local politics, and while at the national level, the relations between Church and state were handled from the top (the pope and only in some cases also the bishops), the activity of these Catholic networks was in lay hands, but it was responsive both to the bishops and to the pope; it had no intention and no way of becoming involved in theological debates.[3] In the next decades, the ties with the local Catholic hierarchies began to loosen in favor of a stronger acknowledgment of the papacy as the sole power in a Church fighting with modernity.

In 1905, the papacy created, or better, reshaped Catholic Action (created in 1868) in Italy, with imitations and replicas in other European states. This was an "army" of lay Catholics who would rely on the pope for their obedience to the Church and for their religious education, and who were thus removed from the influence of the national youth organizations typical of the totalitarian regimes (especially in Italy and Germany). In the 1930s and 1940s, Catholic Action became a mass organization, controlled by the papacy and indirectly by the bishops. Clerical associations like Opus Dei in Spain and the Legionaries of Christ in Mexico followed their own course in fighting (before, during, and after the civil wars) against the modern, anti-Catholic, and nationalist political forces in those countries.[4]

The political mobilization of the Catholic Church between the end of the World War II and the beginning of the Cold War pushed the old elites of Catholicism to conquer political power in many European countries, such as Italy, France, Belgium, the Netherlands, Austria—"the unlikely winner of the post-World War II."[5] These European Catholics were politically engaged in parties marked by a mass membership, with highly centralized, informal decision-making structure—parties with a secular and nonconfessional or interconfessional party image. The party elite had a mostly secular culture, with marginal or no role for clerics; it was a leadership made of middle-class, liberal-moderate lay Catholics, in a party platform engaged in issues that have no clear-cut confessional connotations.

The global détente in the 1970s put an end to the Church's need for mass appeal in both antifascist and anticommunist social and political organizations controlled by the bishops. From the cradle of Catholic Action, there split off silently but steadily a long series of new Catholic movements: Focolari, Comunione e Liberazione, Comunità di Sant'Egidio, and so on. On one side, this hemorrhage gravely weakened the "old army" of Azione Cattolica, whose political and social role lost most of its weight. On the other side, these new movements began to constitute, from the late 1970s on, the "elite troops" of the Catholic Church in dealing in a more identity-driven way with social and economic issues in the Western world.[6] Between the end of the 1970s and the beginning of the 1980s, the attempt is visible in some of the new movements at the same time to claim legitimacy from Vatican II and to take distance from the tumultuous post–Vatican II period.[7]

The movements as such had no role among the participants at Vatican II or in the final documents of the Council, but from the 1980s on, they had recourse to the often-repudiated "spirit of Vatican II," as they had no opportunity to find much support in the conciliar texts themselves.[8] This self-labeling and self-definition of the movements as the purest fruit of Vatican II is one of the most effective manifestations of the "Vatican II nominalism" typical of John Paul II's pontificate. Thus, the new Catholic movements received much support from John Paul II's plan for a "new evangelization" in Europe.[9] Benedict XVI praised the movements, but with less enthusiasm and more awareness of the theological and ecclesiological implications of their activism for the Church as an institution.[10]

Now, at the beginning of the twenty-first century, it is clear that this phenomenon shares much of the "revenge-of-God" weltanschauung, an outlook that is coming to prominence in the monotheistic religions.[11] The debate about the Catholic movements is polarized between supporters and detractors. Supporters acclaim their evangelical lifestyle as a refuge from the chill winds of individualism dominant in the Western world and their creative contribution to the life of the Church, seeing them as having theological roots in Vatican II. Opponents focus instead on the alleged psychological and sociological features of these new movements:

sectarianism, tough leadership style, encouraged endogamy, para-noid anti-intellectualism, and hyperpartisanship.

THE IMPACT OF THE MOVEMENTS ON FREEDOM IN THE LOCAL CATHOLIC CHURCHES

The issue is that new Catholic movements have made the Church more plural and less pluralistic at the same time. This can be seen in the local churches where the movements are more rooted and active.

Vatican II made an epoch-making shift not only at the theoretical level of the ecclesiological debate, but called also for a change in the structure of the Church: from a top-down system of Church structure to a more communional, collegial, and synodal form of the Church. That assumed also a new model of relationship between all the members of the Church: the pope, bishops, clergy, and laity, and between Rome and the local churches. If Vatican II spent much time in addressing collegiality at the top level (the pope and the bishops in collegium), Vatican II spent less time but nevertheless implied a new model of way of being Church also at the local level. That promised a new life for institutions such as synods, provincial councils, and plenary councils that had been largely forgotten in most of European Catholicism since the seventeenth century, but very much practiced in nineteenth-century American Catholicism (let's just think of the plenary councils of Baltimore up to 1884). But that was a promise also of new institutions at the very local level such as new councils and boards at the diocesan and parish level.[12]

In the mind of Vatican II, these institutions were supposed to redress the balance of power within the local church, stressing the ordinary powers of bishops alongside the pope's extraordinary powers in the government of dioceses and enabling the participation of laity to the life of local churches, not just through liturgy and social action, but also through taking part in the theological reception of Vatican II.[13]

Some important but little considered factors have influenced this ongoing process. On one hand, the secularization and the new self-consciousness of the laity gave a considerable push to the weakening of the power of clergy and bishops. On the other, the rise of the movements was not only a reaction against secularization along the lines of John Paul II's slogan of "new evangelization," but also a reaction of the new laity as so-called parvenus against the old elite within the Catholic Church.[14]

It is time to notice that this pivotal shift in the life of Catholicism had a negative impact on the development of collegiality and synodality in the Church at the local level. In the last three decades, the practical ecclesiology of the movements has initiated the end of the bishop- and clergy-led local church—something Vatican II had in mind and prepared. But this step has not been in the direction of a more participatory local church. Rather the movements have replaced the participatory model with a more leader-driven model of Christian community, where inner diversity is, paradoxically, far less present and welcome than in the past. For example, after the post–Vatican II wave of diocesan synods in Italy and elsewhere, the celebration of these key events within the local churches has become very uncommon in the last twenty years. The need for debate between laity and clergy—so strongly felt in the 1960s and 1970s—has been replaced by the creation of strong, personal ties between the bishops and the leaders of the movements at the diocesan level. This partition of the local church is graphically represented in liturgies celebrated separately behind closed doors by different communities (especially the Neocatechumenate).

Within the movements, the need for free speech inside the Church—strongly represented by the twenty centuries of local councils and synods and by the very example of Vatican II, but also by the late institutional and theological development of Catholic Action—is often dismissed as a concession to current social and political taste, and is seen as jeopardizing their new Catholic way of living within the social community.[15]

This negative and pugnacious weltanschauung has peculiar effects on the shape of the new movements. Given the emphasis on the coherence of the group and on its success in perpetuating itself in face of a world perceived as secularist and hostile, the spiritual needs of the less "employable" members of the community easily become marginal both within the movement and within the local church.

When offered this new model of obedient and active Catholicism, local bishops rarely grasp the movements' long-term challenge to the catholic (in the sense of big-tent and plural) set-up of the local church. Driven by the need to fight back secularization at all costs, bishops and clergy tend to perceive the movements as "the real Church," as the ultimate asset for the counterattack against the crisis of authority of Catholicism. The creation of networks of Catholic welfare and the protection of vested interests attached to this volunteerism give the movements active in this area a political, economic, and moral power that few people dare to question as regards its relations with the role of individual Christians in the Church and in society at large.

The rest of the local church and the Catholics not active in the movements are left in a sort of dead zone between this new, front-page Catholicism and the outer world. In a sense, the rise of the movements has re-created within the Catholic Church the medieval *duo genera christianorum* (two types of Christian faithful): a Church in which the distinction between the power holders on one side and the subjects on the other side is clear. The movements' founders and their successors are held up as examples of the new *ecclesia docens* (the teaching Church) against a once again patronized lay Church that is supposed to be the *ecclesia discens* (the learning Church).

At the local and diocesan level, the important distinction is often no longer between clerics and laypeople, but between "movement-belonging Catholics" (in whom the individualism of contemporary Western culture is accommodated through the creation of a variety of different movements for different tastes) and "ordinary, loose Catholics" (whose cultural, social, and moral subjectivity is considered the definitive victory of secularization over the old, comforting, yet gone "shepherd-leading-sheep Catholicism").[16]

THE IMPACT AT THE LEVEL OF THE UNIVERSAL CHURCH

At the universal level, the effects of the new movements on freedom within the Catholic Church are no less critical. One of the roots of the success of the movements is their embrace of the ecclesiology of the universal Church (pushed by Cardinal Ratzinger from the mid-1980s) and their rejection of the ecclesiology of the local church.[17] Besides all the elements that distinguish one movement from another, one key point constitutes the basic ecclesiology of most of them: the ideological acknowledgment of the pope as their only real pastor, almost the *episcopus episcoporum* or *episcopus universalis* of the nineteenth-century ultramontanists.

This globalized ecclesiology, which acts as an undeclared repudiation of Vatican II collegiality and goes even beyond Vatican I–style infallibility,[18] is at the core of some of the new movements' identity. It has heavy implications for the issue of freedom in the Church. The twentieth-century struggle to rediscover the ancient patristic conciliar and synodal tradition in the Church has had a short life. The post–Vatican II, antimodern anguish embodied by the movements has contributed to the failure of the conciliar and synodal institutions in the Church and to the suppression of subsidiarity in the relations between Rome and the local churches, in favor of a modernistic presidential style of leadership that is not traditional and not Catholic.

This latter element does not derive from the development of ecclesiology in the twentieth century or from the great ecclesiological tradition from the late second century on. Rather, it represents the appropriation by the Catholic Church in Europe of some features of antiliberal political culture. This Jacobin attitude of the new elites within the Catholic Church explains the movements' refusal to address the most debated issues in the Church today (sexual ethics, inculturation, ecumenism, and interreligious dialogue) and reflects their and their leaders' refusal to enter a theological debate about the Vatican's policies and their enforcement.[19]

Their increasingly important presence in the institutions of the Roman Curia and their efforts to establish institutions of higher education in Rome tells much about their success in creating a "Roman nest," which is necessary in order to have a voice and a face inside the very heart of universal Catholic Church government. The movements' apparently vast financial resources and the esteem with which they are held in the Catholic mainstream are creating inside the Vatican a fierce market of vocations. The most prestigious universities, such as the Gregorian, are now fighting with the new movements' academically anemic but politically stronger universities and seminaries, which educate priests for the movements' needs around the world.

Surprisingly, though, the ecclesiology of some of the movements embodies a Catholic identity that draws much of its identity from the symbolism of the monarchical papacy, but that also is successful in catholicizing a rather Protestant conception of the Church: a community rich in charisms but with no intermediate level (episcopate, clergy, theologians) between the founder-leader (the pope) and the base (the individual faithful).[20] In this respect, it remains to be seen how the new European-based Catholic movements will contribute to the vitality of theological debate within a Church facing the intellectual challenges of bringing the gospel to the contemporary world. But adaptation is part of the very history of the movements.

The institutionalization of the movements in the body of the Roman Church has come a long way. The juridical status of each of them differs. They represent the richness and the variety of the spiritual traditions within contemporary Catholicism, and in this sense, they are a true manifestation of freedom. But this freedom is given only to the members of the movements, and it comes at the expense, not only of the old Church elites, but of the unorganized laity.

It is fair to say that the role the movements have acquired in the Catholic Church is not helping to foster debate within the Church. On the contrary, it often strengthens anti-intellectual sentiment and rebuffs calls for the freedom of individual, "unlabeled" Catholics within Catholicism.

A SETBACK FOR FREEDOM IN THE CHURCH?

Undoubtedly, the phenomenon of the new Catholic movements represents a new face on the relations between the faithful and the ecclesiastical hierarchy. The blessing given by the papacy and the bishops to the new movements should not cause us to forget how, at the beginning of their history in the 1960s and

1970s, the founders and members of these movements struggled with the hierarchy in order to get permission to act as Catholics outside of the institutional and recognized Catholic lay associations. The new style of leadership, the lay identity of the leaders, their mission to reach out to a new society, and their early independence of clerical authority made for an uneasy relationship among the movements, the bishops, and the Vatican—at least until the mid-1970s. Carried on the wave of 1968 in Europe and America, the movements represented the long-awaited chance (especially in Italy) for a revolutionary *prise de parole* inside the Catholic Church.[21]

But this fight for freedom inside the Catholic Church waged by the new movements—sometimes as insiders, sometimes *against* the institutional establishment and *for* a new model of organized Catholicism—soon turned into the slow but steady development of a new kind of movement Catholicism, which has given this network of communities and movements the same kind of power in the Church that they questioned and fought against immediately after Vatican II. For the members of the movements, freedom in the Church has expanded significantly. Since they are not under ecclesiastical surveillance anymore, their members enjoy considerable liberty in terms of self-government and independence from the institution, liturgical creativity, autonomy of pastoral projects, and social and economic entrepreneurship. On the other hand, the movements tend to form inner communities in order to maintain spiritual warmth and to meet their spiritual and material needs, causing a selection of the members also based on their capability to protect the group identity and to perform the group's mission.

The need for these movements to compete aggressively on the dynamic "market" of Catholic identities manifests itself with the call for an intense and high-cost activism in order to carry out the mission of the community inside the Church. In some cases, this comes at the price of the spiritual and intellectual freedom of the members. The criticisms against the psychological environment in some Catholic groups are not just the fruit of the disappointment of former members. It is a fact that the selection of the members of movements and communities involves not only the ideological and theological personality of the faithful, but also their willingness to devote their entire life—family life, social relations, job opportunities, weltanschauung—to the movement's mission. Often this attitude has been criticized not only because of the sect-like pattern, but also based on a veiled neo-Pelagianism.[22] The minor role of theological reflection in these communities and in the members' education reflects this attitude, as does the refusal to share the language of the old Catholic elites and the adoption instead of an idiom of social action, allegiance to the community, and proud obedience to the pope and to the official teaching of the Church.

This lay mobilization of the Catholic Church for the *reconquista* of the contemporary world leaves often little room for the exercise of freedom inside the movements. While the movements have enhanced the new media-friendly face of world Catholicism, community Catholicism is quite different from Catholicism as a communion. It is enacted in a Church made up of small communities that are highly committed to sharing their members' faith and in making their faith visible and effective, but also to silencing the voices that jeopardize the ticket mentality.[23] Harmony becomes far more important than pluralism; obedience to the leader overrides spiritual freedom; "sound-bite" theology replaces the daily contact with the Bible and with theology as an intellectual effort to read the gospel in the world as it is.

Vatican II is the Council that introduced religious freedom as correlated both to human dignity and to the freedom of the Church. The Council's ecclesiology opened the gates to the future, toward a Church capable of addressing the issue of balance of power within itself and of solving the contradictions between its liturgical-communional identity and an overwhelming inherited ancien régime institutional framework.

After Vatican II, the institutional framework somehow changed and the supremacy of bishops and clergy has been reduced, but this change did not create new balances and new room for freedom in the Church. After the shock of 1968, Catholicism seems to be more and more afraid of freedom in the Church. A major part of the new Catholic movements embodies reaction to this shock and a spirit of fear.

The rise of the new movements is leading to a Church that is effectively no longer run by bishops and clergy (as it was in Tridentine

Catholicism), but is not renewed by a participatory and theologically educated laity either (as the mid-twentieth century theology of the laity dreamed). Rather we see a new alliance between a hyperactive papacy and a highly motivated and mobilized spectrum of movements strongly tied to the pope as the symbolic badge of theological orthodoxy. This could mean the precipitous end of Vatican II's attempt to reconcile Catholicism with the ancient tradition of councils and synods governing the Catholic Church, with democratic, human-rights-based, and participative culture.

In this sense, the fight of John Paul II and Benedict XVI against liberalism brought with itself the dismissal of real concerns for a genuinely liberal issue, that is, psychological and spiritual freedom of the human person even in the Church. From the beginning of John Paul II's pontificate, the new Catholic movements had success and endorsement by the official teaching of the Church and especially by the pope himself. With John Paul II, Paul VI's prudence regarding the new Catholic movements was no longer. Benedict XVI continued the policy of approval of the new Catholic movements inaugurated by his predecessor, aptly inserting his view of the new Catholic movements into his ecclesiology of the Church in modernity as a "small flock." The emergencies, first of the struggle against Communism, and then of the new evangelization, seemed to be more important than other considerations.

SOCIOLOGICAL AND PSYCHOLOGICAL DYNAMICS AND THE NEW CATHOLIC MOVEMENTS

Growing concerns from observers within the Church and from outside about the spiritual climate in some Catholic movements emerged from the world of polemical pamphlets written with the zeal of the convert by former members of the movements, and finally found their way to the papacy with Francis. In November 2014, Pope Francis reminded the movements of the importance of respect of individual freedom:

A further issue concerns the way of welcoming and accompanying men and women of today, in particular, the youth. We are part of a wounded humanity—and we must be honest in saying this—in which all of the educational institutions, especially the most important one, the family, are experiencing grave difficulties almost everywhere in the world. Men and women today experience serious identity problems and have difficulty making proper choices; as a result, they tend to be conditioned and to delegate important decisions about their own lives to others. We need to resist the temptation of usurping individual freedom, of directing them without allowing for their growth in genuine maturity. Every person has their own time, their own path, and we must accompany this journey. Moral or spiritual progress which manipulates a person's immaturity is only an apparent success, and one destined to fail. It is better to achieve less and move forward without seeking attention.[24]

Pope Francis's words represent here a real departure from a silent consensus in the Church about a previously ignored issue. The real flourishing of the new Catholic movements started only after Vatican II and with an implicit dismissal of some basic markers of modern anthropology as it was understood at Vatican II—first of all the sovereignty of human conscience. But bigger changes in the relationship between the Church and the world overshadowed the issues related to the growth of small communities in the Church. A first decisive element in this transition was the change of paradigm in Catholic ecclesiology.[25] Post–Vatican II policy with its emphasis on the laity made the classical distinction between the *duo genera christianorum*—clergy and laity—look rather dated. It also upset the carefully worded balance of powers within the Church between pope and bishops set forth in Vatican II. The new Catholic movements took that window of opportunity to protect their own community ecclesiology, thus neglecting the local dimension of the communion of the Church and choosing the universal Church and its symbol, the pope, as the first and last controller of their catholicity—just as the mendicant orders did in the Middle Ages.[26] In that process, the movements were one of the winners of the post–Vatican II power struggle in the Catholic Church, of which the final results were the undermining of the bishops' authority and the despair of the unorganized laity in some local churches.

With the defeat of the unorganized laity vis-à-vis the new movements came also the dismissal of some basic concerns for the respect of individual freedom in ecclesial groups—freedom that was much more visible and therefore less at risk in the Tridentine, territorial, parish-based Catholicism. There is no way back to that monolithic, territorial, institutional Catholicism typical of European Christendom. But now that movements in the Church have stabilized their presence in the Church and made Catholicism a Church-movement much more than before, it is time to reexamine the relationship among the differences between the sociological and psychological dynamics of a parish-based, territorial Church and the sociological and psychological dynamics of Catholic movements and intentional communities.[27]

Notes

1. On the passage of the laity from preconciliar Catholic Action to the laity in the Church of Vatican II for Europe and Italy, see Massimo Faggioli, *Sorting Out Catholicism: A Brief History of the New Ecclesial Movements* (Collegeville, MN: Liturgical, 2014); for the United States, see James M. O'Toole, *The Faithful: A History of Catholics in America* (Cambridge, MA: Belknap Press of Harvard University Press, 2008), 144–265.

2. See Angelica Steinmaus-Pollak, *Das als katholische Aktion organisierte Laienapostolat: Geschichte seiner Theorie und seiner kirchenrechtlichen Praxis in Deutschland* (Würzburg: Echter, 1988); Yvon Tranvouez, *Catholiques d'abord: approches du mouvement catholique en France (XIXe–XXe siècle)* (Paris: Éditions Ouvrières, 1988); Gérard Cholvy, *Histoire des organisations et mouvements chrétiens de jeunesse en France (XIXe-XXe siècle)* (Paris: Cerf, 1999), 111–47; Andreas Wollasch, *Der Katholische Fürsorgeverein für Mädchen, Frauen und Kinder (1899–1945)* (Freiburg i.B.: Lambertus, 1991).

3. See Liliana Ferrari, *Una storia dell'Azione cattolica. Gli ordinamenti statutari da Pio XI a Pio XII* (Genoa: Marietti, 1989).

4. See John L. Allen Jr., *Opus Dei* (New York: Doubleday, 2005); see also Guy Hermet, *Les catholiques dans l'Espagne franquiste*, vol. 1

(Paris: Presses de la Fondation Nationale des Sciences Politiques, 1980–1981), 231–46; Amadeo de Fuenmayor, Valentín Gomez Iglesias, and José Luis Illanes, *El itinerario juridico del Opus Dei. Historia y defensa de un carisma* (Pamplona: Univ. de Navarra, 1989); Jason Berry, Gerald Renner, *Vows of Silence: The Abuse of Power in the Papacy of John Paul II* (New York: Free Press, 2004); Joan Josep Matas Pastor, "Origen y desarrollo de los Cursillos de Cristianidad (1949–1975)," *Hispania Sacra* 52, no. 106 (2000): 719–42.

    5. See Wolfram Kaiser, *Christian Democracy and the Origins of European Union* (Cambridge, UK: Cambridge University Press, 2011), 163–90.

    6. See Enzo M. Fondi, Michele Zanzucchi, *Un popolo nato dal Vangelo: Chiara Lubich e i Focolari* (Cinisello B.: San Paolo, 2003); Massimo Camisasca, *Comunione e Liberazione: Le origini (1954–1968)*, foreword by Card. Joseph Ratzinger (Cinisello B.: San Paolo, 2001).

    7. This was especially the positioning of Comunione e Liberazione in Italy in the Church of John Paul II.

    8. See *History of Council Vatican II*, vol. 4, *Church as Communion: Third Period and Intersession, September 1964–September 1965*, ed. G. Alberigo and J. Komonchak (Maryknoll, NY: Orbis, 2004); Barbara Zadra, *I movimenti ecclesiali e i loro statuti* (Rome: Pontificia Università Gregriana, 1997), 7–21.

    9. See Massimo Faggioli, "Tra chiesa territoriale e chiese personali: I movimenti ecclesiali nel post-concilio Vaticano II," *Cristianesimo nella Storia* 24 (2003): 677–704.

    10. See Joseph Card. Ratzinger with Vittorio Messori, *The Ratzinger Report* (San Francisco: Ignatius, 1995); Joseph Card. Ratzinger with Peter Seewald, *Salt of the Earth: Christianity and the Catholic Church at the End of the Millennium* (San Francisco: Ignatius, 1997); Joseph Ratzinger, "I movimenti ecclesiali e la loro collocazione teologica," in *I movimenti nella chiesa* (Vatican City: Libreria Editrice Vaticana, 1999), 23–51. Translated as *Movements in the Church: Proceedings of the World Congress of the Ecclesial Movements, Rome, 27–29 May 1998* (Vatican City: Pontificium Consilium pro Laicis, 1999); Joseph Ratzinger, *Nuove irruzioni dello spirito: i movimenti nella Chiesa* (Cinisello B.: San Paolo, 2006).

    11. See Gilles Kepel, *The Revenge of God: The Resurgence of Islam, Christianity, and Judaism in the Modern World* (University Park, PA: Pennsylvania State University Press, 1994); R. Scott Appleby and Emmanuel Sivan, *Strong Religion: The Rise of Fundamentalisms around the World* (Chicago: University of Chicago Press, 2003).

    12. See *Synod and Synodality: Theology, History, Canon Law and*

Ecumenism in New Contact, ed. Alberto Melloni and Silvia Scatena (Münster: LIT, 2005).

13. See Massimo Faggioli, *Il vescovo e il concilio. Modello episcopale e aggiornamento al Vaticano II* (Bologna: Il Mulino, 2005).

14. For the historical ties between the episcopate, the clergy, and the social elites in Europe, see Joseph Bergin, "L'Europe des Évêques au temps de la réforme catholique," *Bibliothèque de l'École des chartes* 154 (1996): 509–31; Claudio Donati, "Vescovi e diocesi d'Italia dall'età post-tridentina alla caduta dell'antico regime," in *Clero e società nell'Italia moderna*, ed. Mario Rosa (Rome-Bari: Laterza, 1992), 321–89; Wolfgang Reinhard, ed., *Power Elites and State Building* (Oxford: Oxford University Press, 1996); Christoph Weber, *Senatus divinus: Verborgene Strukturen im Kardinalskollegium der frühen Neuzeit (1500–1800)* (Frankfurt a.M.: Peter Lang, 1996); Erwin Gatz, ed., *Die Bischöfe der deutschsprachigen Länder, 1785/1803 bis 1945: Ein biographisches Lexikon* (Berlin: Duncker & Humblot, 1983).

15. See Massimo Faggioli, "Chiese locali ed ecclesiologia prima e dopo il concilio di Trento," in *Storia della Chiesa in Europa tra ordinamento politico-amministrativo e strutture ecclesiastiche*, ed. Luciano Vaccaro (Brescia: Morcelliana, 2005), 197–213.

16. See Danièle Hervieu-Léger, *Le pèlerin et le converti: la religion en mouvement* (Paris: Flammarion, 1999).

17. See Massimo Faggioli, "Prassi e norme relative alle conferenze episcopali tra concilio Vaticano II e post-concilio (1959–1998)," in Melloni and Scatena, *Synod and Synodality*, 265–96.

18. See Hermann Joseph Pottmeyer, *Towards a Papacy in Communion: Perspectives from Vatican Councils I & II* (New York: Crossroad, 1998); John R. Quinn, *The Reform of the Papacy* (New York: Herder & Herder, 2000).

19. See Shmuel N. Eisenstadt, *Fundamentalism, Sectarianism, and Revolution: The Jacobin Dimension of Modernity* (Cambridge: Cambridge University Press, 1999).

20. See Mark A. Noll and Carolyn Nystrom, *Is the Reformation Over? An Evangelical Assessment of Contemporary Roman Catholicism* (Grand Rapids: Baker, 2005).

21. See Michel de Certeau, *The Capture of Speech and Other Political Writings* (Minneapolis: University of Minnesota Press, 1997).

22. See *A colloquio con Dossetti e Lazzati: Intervista di Leopoldo Elia e Pietro Scoppola (19 novembre 1984)* (Bologna: Il Mulino, 2003).

23. See Theodor W. Adorno et al., *The Authoritarian Personality* (New York: Harper, 1950); Elias Canetti, *Crowds and Power*, trans. Carol Stewart (New York: Continuum, 1973).

24. Pope Francis, Address to Participants in the Third World Congress of Ecclesial Movements and New Communities, November 22, 2014, http://w2.vatican.va/content/francesco/en/speeches/2014/november/documents/papa-francesco_20141122_convegno-movimenti-ecclesiali.html.

25. See Richard P. McBrien, *The Church: The Evolution of Catholicism* (New York: Harper, 2008), 182–92 and 345–49.

26. See Giovanni Miccoli, *Chiesa gregoriana: Ricerche sulla riforma del secolo XI* (Rome: Edizioni di Storia e Letteratura, 1999), 1–58.

27. About this, see Alessandro Rovello, *La morale e i movimenti ecclesiali* (Bologna: EDB, 2013).

7

POPE FRANCIS AND THE CATHOLIC MOVEMENTS

A New Ecclesiological Appraisal

A JESUIT POPE AND THE NEW MOVEMENTS

IN THE DAYS BEFORE the conclave, even before Francis's election, some journalists reported that as bishop in Argentina, Bergoglio had become close to the Communion and Liberation (CL) movement over the years.[1] The election of Francis was, however, disappointing news for some members of the movement. In Italy, where Communion and Liberation witnessed the defeat of their candidate, the cardinal archbishop of Milan Angelo Scola, members of CL—politically the most visible of all Catholic movements in Italy—tried to present themselves as very familiar with the new pope.[2] The transition from one pontificate to another is an extremely delicate moment for the positioning of the new Catholic movements. Since the rise of the movements in the 1980s, conclaves have been seen as tests of the political power of the movements in Church politics, and especially in its most important moments.[3]

Facing the surprising outcome of the conclave of March 2013, CL's sympathizers in Italy may have overstated the case for the closeness between Bergoglio and their movement. But this is interesting not only for a political analysis of the positioning of the Catholic movements at the beginning of a new pontificate; there is a theological point to be made here. Those who tried to tie Pope Francis to his relationship with CL when he was still an archbishop underestimated the discontinuities between Bergoglio the archbishop of Buenos Aires and Francis the Bishop of Rome—which is one of the great hermeneutical keys to interpreting Francis's pontificate and the papacy in general.[4] If Bergoglio's life in Argentina is relevant to understanding Pope Francis, his relationship with the movements as a Jesuit and as a bishop are probably less indicative of the trajectories of the pontificate about the movements.

The second element of Bergoglio's biography that might be misleading for those who look for a continuity between Francis's and his predecessors' approach to the issue of the new movements is his being a member of the Society of Jesus—the first Jesuit pope. Identified sometimes as the model par excellence of a movement within the Catholic Church, the Society of Jesus is undoubtedly part of the long history of the quest for new ways of living in the Church (a history beginning with the wave of the new mendicant orders in medieval Europe). But it is also true that in these last fifty years of Church history, the Jesuits remained engaged in a Church and embodied a theology that is fully conciliar and postconciliar: Vatican II was a key moment in the evolution of the Jesuits, and a departure from a pre–Vatican II Society of Jesus toward a kind of Catholicism that does not fit completely the description of Catholicism offered by the new Catholic movements—especially when it comes to the relationship between the Jesuits and modern culture and the contribution of the Jesuits to the intellectual life of the Catholic Church.[5]

In other words, on the one hand, the postconciliar identity of the Society of Jesus is much more marked by the theology of Vatican II than by the freedom given by Vatican II to the new Catholic movements to interpret Catholicism; on the other hand, the relationship between Jorge Mario Bergoglio and the Society of Jesus is one of the most fascinating and complex issues to study in order to understand Francis's pontificate.[6] In this sense, the biographical element does not tell us something clearly indicated about Francis and the new Catholic movements—the most important part of Francis's biography to consider might not be his formation and identity as a member of the Society of Jesus. The best way to approach the issue of Francis and the movement is to look at what Francis as a pope said to them.

FRANCIS AND THE NEW MOVEMENTS: A SHIFT FROM JOHN PAUL II AND BENEDICT XVI

There is an abundant literature on the meetings and audiences between the popes and the new ecclesial movements, both in general and individually. All these messages sent by the pope to these new important voices in the Church are public in the sense that they are not secret: the pope speaks to the movements while he speaks to the whole Church that the movements are part of, even if they do not represent the whole Church. But it is also true that the "script" of the meetings between the popes and the movements has been, in recent times (that is, since John Paul II), part of a carefully staged scene of two new protagonists on the stage: the new, post–Vatican II papacy in the world of global media, and the new, post–Vatican II lay movements in world Catholicism. Pope Francis did not reject this stage, as he rejected little of the rest of the Vatican "machine": he is a pope engaging the new ecclesial movements as part of a renewed relationship between the Church and the world. But Francis performed an interesting script that is partly new and different from the previous pontificates.

On May 19, 2013, on Pentecost, two months after his election, Pope Francis met representatives of the new ecclesial movements in St. Peter's Square. During the Saturday evening vigil, Francis answered questions from the faithful in the square. In answering one question, he presented his vision of the Church but also of his vision of life in a movement:

> Times of crisis, like the one we are living through...is [*sic*] not merely an economic crisis. It is not a crisis of culture. It is a human crisis: it is the human person that

is in crisis! Man himself is in danger of being destroyed! But man is the image of God! This is why it is a profound crisis! At this time of crisis we cannot be concerned solely with ourselves, withdrawing into loneliness, discouragement and a sense of powerlessness in the face of problems. Please do not withdraw into yourselves! This is a danger: we shut ourselves up in the parish, with our friends, within the movement, with the like-minded... but do you know what happens? When the Church becomes closed, she becomes an ailing Church, she falls ill! That is a danger. Nevertheless we lock ourselves up in our parish, among our friends, in our movement, with people who think as we do...but do you know what happens? When the Church is closed, she falls sick, she falls sick. Think of a room that has been closed for a year. When you go into it there is a smell of damp, many things are wrong with it. A Church closed in on herself is the same, a sick Church.[7]

Francis warned against the temptation to use the movement as a refuge where the like-minded can withdraw. In this sense, Francis's ecclesiology of a Church open to the world also extends to the ecclesiology of the new ecclesial movements: the Church is a movement but the movements are not the Church. The diminished emphasis, in Francis's pontificate, on the danger of secularization and modernity entailed a view of the ecclesial movements as being more normal, less privileged than they were used to under John Paul II and Benedict XVI.

The movements certainly play a specific role in Francis's ecclesiology. During the homily at mass on May 20, 2013, Pope Francis commented the reading from Acts and pointed out "three words linked to the working of the Holy Spirit: newness, harmony and mission":

Only the Spirit can awaken diversity, plurality and multiplicity, while at the same time building unity. Here too, when we are the ones who try to create diversity and close ourselves up in what makes us different and other, we bring division. When we are the ones who want to build unity in accordance with our human plans, we end up creating uniformity, standardization. But if instead we let ourselves be guided by the Spirit, richness, variety and diversity never become a source of conflict, because he impels us to experience variety within the communion of the Church. Journeying together in the Church, under the guidance of her pastors who possess a special charism and ministry, is a sign of the working of the Holy Spirit. Having a sense of the Church is something fundamental for every Christian, every community and every movement. It is the Church which brings Christ to me, and me to Christ; parallel journeys are very dangerous! When we venture beyond the Church's teaching and community— the Apostle John tells us in his Second Letter—and do not remain in them, we are not one with the God of Jesus Christ (cf. 2 John 9). So let us ask ourselves: Am I open to the harmony of the Holy Spirit, overcoming every form of exclusivity? Do I let myself be guided by him, living in the Church and with the Church?[8]

The interesting emphasis here is on the role of the hierarchy for the movements for the sake of the unity of the Church: the movements cannot be about *exclusivity*. But even more important is Francis's cautioning against the risk of building unhealthy relationships between movements and the rest of the Church. Francis is very clear in letting the movements be what they need to be, but he also warns them about the dangers of "parallel journeys." This is important because it represents a departure from the emphasis of his predecessors John Paul II and Benedict XVI on some kind of autonomy of the movements from the Church hierarchy—but not autonomy from the papacy, of course.[9] For example, on June 3, 2006, on the vigil of Pentecost, at the meeting with the ecclesial movements and new communities, Benedict XVI warned bishops not to set limits to the movements: "Pastors must be careful not to extinguish the Spirit and you will not cease to bring your gifts to the entire community."[10]

An interesting ecclesiological element regarding the movements in the Church is about the role of the parish and the Tridentine territorial structure. During the pontificates of John Paul II and Benedict XVI, the preference given to the movements came, especially in some local churches, at the expense of the role of the parish (and of the religious orders). In Francis's apostolic exhortation *Evangelii Gaudium* (November 24, 2013), the parish is given back its proper role:

> 28. The parish is not an outdated institution; precisely because it possesses great flexibility, it can assume quite different contours depending on the openness and missionary creativity of the pastor and the community. While certainly not the only institution which evangelizes, if the parish proves capable of self-renewal and constant adaptivity, it continues to be "the Church living in the midst of the homes of her sons and daughters."...It is a community of communities, a sanctuary where the thirsty come to drink in the midst of their journey, and a centre of constant missionary outreach. We must admit, though, that the call to review and renew our parishes has not yet sufficed to bring them nearer to people, to make them environments of living communion and participation, and to make them completely mission-oriented.
>
> 29. Other Church institutions, basic communities and small communities, movements, and forms of association are a source of enrichment for the Church, raised up by the Spirit for evangelizing different areas and sectors. Frequently they bring a new evangelizing fervor and a new capacity for dialogue with the world whereby the Church is renewed. But it will prove beneficial for them not to lose contact with the rich reality of the local parish and to participate readily in the overall pastoral activity of the particular Church. This kind of integration will prevent them from concentrating only on part of the Gospel or the Church, or becoming nomads without roots.[11]

Here Francis is calling the movements to "participate readily in the overall pastoral activity of the particular Church." Rootedness in the Church requires "integration" in the form of "participation" in the larger community. The reminder sent to the movements about the need to maintain contact with the local parish is part of Francis's ecclesiology, but also of the pastoral experience of Jorge Mario Bergoglio, the Jesuit educator and then archbishop of Buenos Aires.

Another new element in Francis's view of the movements is the reinclusion in the pope's pastoral care of movements that were seen with suspicion for a long time under John Paul II and Benedict XVI. In January 2014, Pope Francis sent a message to the Thirteenth Inter-ecclesial Meeting of the Basic Ecclesial Communities taking place in Brazil. Francis sent these communities a brief message quoting *Evangelii Gaudium* paragraph 29 about the relationship between movement and local church.[12] The remarkable fact is that it was the first time a pope sent a message to the base ecclesial communities in Latin America, which for a long time were suspected of being too close to (or even of being expressions of) liberation theology. Francis's understanding of the movements in the Church is more inclusive because his whole ecclesiology is more inclusive. That is why Francis's messages to the movements always contain an invitation to these new ecclesial groups to foster inclusiveness and unity in diversity in the Church.

Francis does not recommend more integration between movement and local church to one particular ecclesial movement, but to all of them. On February 1, 2014, in a meeting with members of the Neocatechumenal Way, Francis invited them to "preserve the communion with the local Churches":

> I would like to give you a few simple recommendations. The first is to take the greatest care to build and preserve *the communion within the particular Churches* where you will go to work. The Way has its own charism, its own dynamic, a gift that like all gifts of the Holy Spirit has a profoundly ecclesial dimension; this means listening to the life of the Churches where your leaders send you, appreciating their riches, suffering through their weaknesses if necessary, and walking together as a single flock under the guidance of the Pastors of the local Churches. Communion is essential: at times it can be better to give up living out in detail what your itinerary would call for,

in order to guarantee unity among the brethren who form one ecclesial community, which you must always feel a part of.[13]

This speech to the Neocatechumenals was probably one of the most straightforward and severe messages of a pope to a new Catholic movement. Everybody could interpret the message about unity and communion in the local churches in light of the tensions between the movement and the local episcopates, in Japan and elsewhere.[14] However, a year later, an audience with the Neocatechumenal Way in March 2015 showed fewer tensions between Francis and the leadership of the movement, which was praised for being an example of a missionary Church:

> You have received the strength to leave everything and depart for a distant land thanks to a way of Christian initiation, lived out in these little communities, where you have rediscovered the immense riches of your Baptism. This is *the Neocatechumenal Way*, a true gift of Providence to the Church of our times, as my Predecessors have already confirmed....So often, in the Church, we have Jesus inside but we don't let him go forth....So often! This is the most important thing to do if we don't want the waters to stagnate in the Church. For years the Way has carried out this *missio ad gentes* among non-Christians for an *implantatio Ecclesiae*, a new presence of the Church, there where the Church does not exist or is no longer capable of reaching people.[15]

Francis's concern for the unity of the Church extends to every church, even to the local church of Rome, his diocese. In the audience of March 8, 2014, to the leaders of the ecclesial movements of the diocese of Rome, he invited them to avoid the danger of building a contraposition between the movements and the parishes.[16]

Francis's ecclesiology is not only an ecclesiology of unity of the Church but also a missionary ecclesiology. It is therefore an ecclesiology for a Church that is engaged in the world—a Church that is not afraid to visibly and openly support those priests who work for justice in social movements. Fr. Luigi Ciotti is one of the most popular Italian priests, known for his work in Libera, an association fighting against the Mafia.[17] For his social activism, Fr. Ciotti had long been viewed with suspicion by the Vatican and the Catholic establishment in Italy. On March 21, 2014, Francis met with him and his association in a parish near the Vatican for a vigil prayer for the victims of the Mafia and their families.[18] That remarkable moment of prayer and civil activism is part of Francis's more inclusive view of the movements in the Church, especially of Catholic social justice movements that often operate together with non-Catholic, non-Christian, or nonreligious social justice movements.

A few months later, in his address to the participants in the world meeting of popular movements, Francis connected his view of the movements with his strong emphasis on social justice:

> Be careful, it is never good to confine a movement in rigid structures, so I say you should keep on meeting. Even worse is the attempt to absorb movements, direct or dominate them—unfettered movements have their own dynamic; nevertheless, yes, we must try to walk together. Here we are in this Old Synod Hall (now there is a new one), and synod means precisely "to walk together." May this be a symbol of the process that you have begun and are carrying forward. Grassroots movements express the urgent need to revitalize our democracies, so often hijacked by innumerable factors. It is impossible to imagine a future for society without the active participation of great majorities as protagonists, and such proactive participation overflows the logical procedures of formal democracy. Moving towards a world of lasting peace and justice calls us to go beyond paternalistic forms of assistance; it calls us to create new forms of participation that include popular movements and invigorate local, national and international governing structures with that torrent of moral energy that springs from including the excluded in the building of a common destiny. And all this with a constructive spirit, without resentment, with love.[19]

In Francis's view of the movements, there is a genuine bio-graphical and personal element that the pope does nothing to hide. In the June 1, 2014, meeting with the members of Renewal in the Holy Spirit at the Olympic stadium of Rome, Francis recalled his first encounter with the movement in a rather personal and peculiar way:

> As you may know—because news gets around—in the first years of the charismatic renewal in Buenos Aires, I didn't care very much for charismatics. I used to think: "They strike me as some kind of samba school!" I didn't share their style of prayer or the many new things which were happening in the Church. Later, I got to know them and I finally realized all the good that the charismatic renewal was doing for the Church. And this story which began with the "samba school" had an unexpected ending: a few months before entering the conclave, I was named the spiritual assistant for the charismatic renewal in Argentina by the Conference of Bishops.[20]

Pope Francis's liturgical style puts him in some distance from the style of Charismatic Catholics, but that also allows him to describe the contribution of the movements to the Church in terms of a *symphonia*, as he did in the address to the Renewal in the Holy Spirit in June 2014:

> When I think of charismatics, I think of the Church herself, but in a particular way: I think of a great orchestra, where all the instruments and voices are different from one another, yet all are needed to create the harmony of the music. Saint Paul speaks of this in the twelfth chapter of the First Letter to the Corinthians. As in an orchestra, no one in the renewal can think of himself or herself as being more important or greater than the others, please! Because when you think of yourselves as more important or greater, disaster is already on the horizon![21]

Freedom in the Spirit, constant renewal, and the risk of excessive planning are identified by Francis as typical of the movements, but they are also part of his ecclesiology:

> You, the people of God, the people of the charismatic renewal, must be careful not to lose the freedom which the Holy Spirit has given you! The danger for the renewal, as our dear Fr. Raniero Cantalamessa often says, is that of getting too organized: the danger of excessive planning. Yes, you need organization, but never lose the grace of letting God be God!...Go out into the streets and evangelize. Proclaim the Gospel. Remember that the Church was born "on the move," that Pentecost morning. Draw close to the poor and touch in their flesh the wounded flesh of Jesus. Let yourselves be guided by the Holy Spirit, in freedom; and please, don't put the Holy Spirit in a cage! Be free! Seek unity in the renewal, the unity which comes from the Trinity![22]

In a meeting with Charismatic Catholics a few months later, Francis developed his ecclesiology of the movements as an ecclesiology of complementarity and of differences, unity in diversity:

> The first is unity in diversity. Uniformity is not Catholic, it is not Christian. Rather, unity in diversity. Catholic unity is different but it is one: this is curious! The cause of diversity is also the cause of unity: the Holy Spirit. The Holy Spirit does two things: he creates unity in diversity. Unity does not imply uniformity; it does not necessarily mean doing everything together or thinking in the same way. Nor does it signify a loss of identity. Unity in diversity is actually the opposite: it involves the joyful recognition and acceptance of the various gifts which the Holy Spirit gives to each one and the placing of these gifts at the service of all members of the Church. It means knowing how to listen, to accept differences, and having the freedom to think differently and express oneself with complete respect towards the

other who is my brother or sister. Do not be afraid of differences!"[23]

Francis's ecclesiology of the new movements is part of his ecumenical ecclesiology. Francis recalled here the visit he paid a few weeks before to a small Pentecostal community near Naples in the summer of 2014 (the first visit of a pope to Pentecostals in Italy, a tiny community that was persecuted during Mussolini's Fascist regime):

> I see that you have among you a very dear friend, Pastor Giovanni Traettino, whom I visited recently. *Catholic Fraternity*, do not forget your origins, do not forget that the Charismatic Renewal is, by its very nature, ecumenical....Spiritual ecumenism is praying and proclaiming together that Jesus is Lord, and coming together to help the poor in all their poverty. This must be done while never forgetting in our day that the blood of Jesus, poured out by many Christian martyrs in various parts of the world, calls us and compels us towards the goal of unity. For persecutors, we are not divided, we are not Lutherans, Orthodox, Evangelicals, Catholics....No! We are one in their eyes! For persecutors we are Christians! They are not interested in anything else. This is the ecumenism of blood that we experience today.[24]

Some movements, like the Community of Sant'Egidio, are particularly close to Francis's agenda and his message on social justice and the poor, as it became evident in the visit of the pope to Sant'Egidio's headquarters in Santa Maria in Trastevere in Rome on June 15, 2014:

> From here, from Santa Maria in Trastevere, I send my greeting to all those who participate in your community in other Countries of the world. I encourage them as well to be friends of God, of the poor and of peace: those who live this way will be blessed in life and will be a blessing for others. In some Countries suffering from war, you seek to keep hope for *peace* alive. Working

for peace doesn't bring quick results, but it is the work of patient artisans who seek that which unites and set aside that which divides, as Saint John XXIII said. More prayer and more dialogue are needed: they're necessary. The world suffocates without dialogue. Dialogue is only possible starting from true identity. I cannot pretend to have a different identity in order to dialogue. No, it isn't possible to dialogue in this way. This is my identity and I dialogue because I'm a person, because I'm a man or a woman; and man and woman have the opportunity to dialogue without negotiating their identity. The world suffocates without dialogue: for this you also make your contribution, in order to promote friendship among religions. Go forth on this path: *prayer, the poor and peace.* And as you walk this path, you help compassion grow in the heart of society—which is the true revolution, that of compassion and tenderness—to cultivate friendship in place of the ghosts of animosity and indifference.[25]

The most significant shift from John Paul II and Benedict XVI is Francis's constant call to the movements to see themselves not as the Church or the paradigm of a new militant Church, but as part of the Catholic Church. Care for the unity of the Church, freshness of the charism, and respect for the freedom of the faithful in the movements—these three elements sum up the recommendations of Francis to the new ecclesial realities during the first two years of his pontificate. Francis offered a most complete version of his vision in the address to the participants in the third world congress of ecclesial movements and new communities on November 22, 2014.

The first element is the preservation of the "freshness of the charism":

The Movements and New Communities that you represent are moving towards a deeper sense of belonging to the Church, a maturity that requires vigilance in the path of daily conversion. This will enable an ever more dynamic and fruitful evangelization. I would like, therefore, to offer you a few suggestions for your journey of faith and ecclesial life. First, it is necessary to preserve the freshness of your charism, never lose that freshness, the freshness of your charism, always renewing the "first love" (cf. Rev 2:4). As time goes by, there is a greater temptation to become comfortable, to become hardened in set ways of doing things, which, while reassuring, are nonetheless sterile.

The second element is a particular care for the wounded humanity that seeks refuge in the movements. Francis warns against the temptation of "usurping individual freedom":

A further issue concerns the way of welcoming and accompanying men and women of today, in particular, the youth. We are part of a wounded humanity—and we must be honest in saying this—in which all of the educational institutions, especially the most important one, the family, are experiencing grave difficulties almost everywhere in the world. Men and women today experience serious identity problems and have difficulty making proper choices; as a result, they tend to be conditioned and to delegate important decisions about their own lives to others. We need to resist the temptation of usurping individual freedom, of directing them without allowing for their growth in genuine maturity. Every person has their own time, their own path, and we must accompany this journey. Moral or spiritual progress which manipulates a person's immaturity is only an apparent success, and one destined to fail. It is better to achieve less and move forward without seeking attention.

Finally, the third element is the importance of communion in the Church:

One other consideration we must never forget is that the most precious good, the seal of the Holy Spirit, is communion. This is the supreme blessing that Jesus won for us on the Cross, the grace which the Risen Christ continually implores for us as he reveals to the Father his glorious wounds, "As you, Father, are in me, and I in you, may they also be in us, so that the world may believe that you have sent me" (John 17:21). For the world to believe that Jesus is Lord, it needs to see communion among Christians. If, on the other hand, the world sees divisions, rivalries, backbiting, the terrorism of gossip, please…if these things are seen, regardless of the cause, how can we evangelize?…In addition, real communion cannot exist in Movements or in New Communities unless these are integrated within the greater communion of our Holy Mother, the hierarchical Church. "The whole is greater than the part" (*Evangelii Gaudium* par. 234–237), and the part only has meaning in relation to the whole. Communion also consists in confronting together and in a united fashion the most pressing questions of our day, such as life, the family, peace, the fight against poverty in all its forms, religious freedom and education. In particular, New Movements and Communities are called to coordinate their efforts in caring for those wounded by a globalized mentality which places consumption at the center, neglecting God and those values which are essential for life. [26]

Communion with the Church—especially with the local church, not only with the hierarchy—was also part of the message of Francis to the members of Communion and Liberation (CL), whose fame in Italy is that of a Catholic movement deeply embedded in the political system and therefore part of the corruption of Italian politics. In the meeting with the seventy thousand members of CL in St. Peter's Square in March 2015, Francis offered his vision of the movement as rooted in the original message of the founder, Fr. Luigi Giussani, but also countered the moralistic Catholicism often associated with the movement.

The privileged place of encounter is the caress of Jesus' mercy regarding my sin. This is why you may have heard me say, several times, that the place for this, the privileged place of the encounter with Jesus Christ is my sin.

The will to respond and to change, which can give rise to a different life, comes thanks to this merciful embrace. Christian morality is not a titanic, voluntary effort, of one who decides to be coherent and who manages to do so, a sort of isolated challenge before the world. No. This is not Christian morality, it is something else. Christian morality is a response, it is the heartfelt response before the surprising, unforeseeable—even "unfair" according to human criteria—mercy of One who knows me, knows my betrayals and loves me just the same, appreciates me, embraces me, calls me anew, hopes in me, has expectations of me. Christian morality is not a never falling down, but an always getting up, thanks to his hand which catches us. This too is the way of the Church: to let the great mercy of God become manifest.[27]

Francis then spoke of the role of charism not only in shaking up the institution of the Church, but also the institutionalization of the movements themselves—thus speaking openly of the typical issue of the Catholic movements in the last (at least) ten centuries of dialectic between charismatic element and institutional element in Catholicism:

Thus the charism is not preserved in a bottle of distilled water! Faithfulness to the charism does not mean "to petrify it"—the devil is the one who "petrifies," do not forget! Faithfulness to the charism does not mean to write it on a parchment and frame it. The reference to the legacy that Don Giussani left you cannot be reduced to a museum of records, of decisions taken, of the rules of conduct. It certainly entails faithfulness to tradition, but faithfulness to tradition, Mahler said, "is not to worship the ashes but to pass on the flame." Don Giussani would never forgive you if you lost the liberty and transformed yourselves into museum guides or worshippers of ashes. Pass on the flame of the memory of that first encounter and be free!...The way of the Church is to leave her walls behind and go in search of those who are distant, on the peripheries, to serve

146

Jesus in every person who is marginalized, abandoned, without faith, disappointed by the Church, a prisoner of one's own selfishness.[28]

Francis's reminder of the danger of exclusivity and self-referentiality for the movements in the Church—especially when they become a label—is very important:

"To go forth" also means to reject self-referentiality, in all its forms. It means knowing how to listen to those who are not like us, learning from everyone, with sincere humility. When we are slaves to self-referentiality we end up cultivating a "labelled spirituality": "I'm a member of CL." This is the label. Then we fall into the thousands of traps offered to us by the pleasure of self-referentiality; by that looking at ourselves in the mirror which leads us to confusion and transforms us into mere impresarios in an NGO.[29]

This speech to CL was less encomiastic than the speeches given by the popes to CL in recent Church history—especially if compared to the preference for CL openly expressed by John Paul II and Benedict XVI. High-ranking members of the movement took notice and expressed their disappointment publicly but honestly: "What the Pope did in his speech is essentially to issue a warning to CL."[30] Overall, the intellectual elite members of CL showed the will to learn from the pope's teaching, trying to identify continuities between their founder, Fr. Giussani, and Pope Francis.[31]

THE NEW MOVEMENTS AND THE UNITY OF THE CHURCH—FIFTY YEARS AFTER VATICAN II

One of the most important Catholic theologians in Italy today, Pierangelo Sequeri, commented on the two important audiences with Catholic movements in those two days of March 2015 (March 6 with Neocatechumenal Way, March 7 with Communion and Liberation) and talked about the impossibility for the movements to become closes enclaves. But he was also talking about the impossibility for the Church to give up the movements.[32] This comment (published in the widely read daily newspaper of the Italian bishops' conference, *Avvenire*) worked as a reassurance for the movements trying to adjust to the Argentine pope, and it said something about the new tone of Francis about the movements, and about the objective convergences between Francis's ecclesiology and the contribution of the movements to Catholicism today. Here, when Francis's pontificate is still unfolding, it is possible only to advance a few hypotheses.

Francis has evidently toned down the previous popes' emphasis on the special role of the movements, but he has not turned cold toward them. Rather, he has pointed out the possible distance between the movements' charismatic gifts and their founders on one side and their later development and real life of the movements on the other side. In this, Francis has said something that is still a taboo for some very young movements, whose founders are in many cases still alive. On the other hand, Pope Francis as a Jesuit knows that the new Catholic movements are facing a challenge similar to the one the religious orders went through during the post–Vatican II period: the delicate operation of balancing the renewal in the spirit of the charisma of the founder with the aggiornamento required of a Church in the modern world.

Francis has chosen a more cautious tone that responds to an appreciation of the role of the movements in global Catholicism, but also fruit of the awareness of the tensions existing between movements and bishops in some countries. In several occasions during the first two years of his pontificate, Francis has spoken to the movements, always inviting them to a more collaborative stance with the rest of the Church, especially with the parishes. It is a significant change from the previous thirty-five years and an acknowledgment of the possible problems in letting the movements act in a structure of the Church that is still very Tridentine, that is, based on ordained ministry and a territorial organization (diocese and parish).

Francis's is not an ecclesiology complacent with the status quo, and even less complacent with clericalism. The movements are a powerful counterbalance to the dominance of a clerical system.

Also because of that, Francis's understanding of the word *move-ment* is very comprehensive: social movements and ecclesial move-ments both belong to a worldview in which *process* is a key word for Francis and his idea of change.[33] The Church as a movement is part of the transition from a modern and Tridentine ecclesial (European) self-understanding to a postmodern, postinstitutional (global) Catholicism.[34] In this sense, one of the most radical depar-tures of Pope Francis from the vocabulary of John Paul II and Benedict XVI about the movements and the Church is the inclu-sion of the popular movements advocating social and economic justice as an integral part of the pope's audience.

But there is also a deep connection between Francis's ecclesi-ology and the movements, in particular with Francis's focus on the *sensus fidei* and the theology of the people. Francis is a pope of the people and not of the elites—another visible difference between Jorge Mario Bergoglio and Joseph Ratzinger. When movements become elites in the Church, we see a clear distance from Francis's ecclesiology, where *communio* ecclesiology and people of God ecclesiology coexist:

> Behind the pope's pastoral style, which is close to the people, stands an entire theology, indeed his mysticism of the people. For him the Church is far more than an organic and hierarchical institution. It is above all the people of God on their way to God, a pilgrim and evan-gelizing people that transcends every—even if neces-sary—institutional expression.[35]

Francis considers the movements as a key part of the missionary identity of a Church whose movements are part of the Church as a people, where there is no elite and no lower class. Francis's messages to the movements are a clear contribution in putting to an end the idea of the *duo genera christianorum*—"two kinds of Christians"—with the movements embodying the new perfect model of being a lay Catholic in the Church. Francis and the new Catholic movements share an idea of Church renewal that criticizes and bypasses clericalism, but at the same time does not advocate for radical changes (such as women's ordination) that are typical of the liberal culture of the northern hemisphere of the world.

Nevertheless, there is a bigger convergence between the pope and the movements, especially with those movements that are focused on mission and evangelization. In the words of his best interpreter and the most important theologian of the pontificate, Cardinal Walter Kasper: "Pope Francis is defined by kerygmatic theology. In this way he is not a covert Franciscan; he is a Jesuit through and through."[36] He is a reformer, but first he is a "renewer." Pope Francis's ecclesiology in *Evangelii Gaudium* cannot be easily framed as a progressive or liberal ecclesiology, but rather a missionary ecclesiology faithful to the message of Vatican II: *renewal/renewed* is used twenty-nine times against the five times of *reform/reformation*. The Catholic movements of the post–Vatican II period are movements not primarily of Church reform, but of Church renewal: this difference plays a role in Francis's understanding of the movements and messages to the movements. Francis's encouragement to the movements to work for unity in the Church is part of his ecclesiology, but also of his honest evaluation of the state of the Catholic Church at fifty years from Vatican II. It is his way to make clear that the ecclesiology of Vatican II and the ecclesiology of the new Catholic movements are two things that do not overlap completely.

Notes

1. John L. Allen Jr., "New Pope, Jesuit Bergoglio, Was Runner-Up in 2005 Conclave," *National Catholic Reporter*, March 3, 2013, http://ncronline.org/blogs/ncr-today/papabile-day-men-who-could-be-pope-13.

2. See the article published the day after Francis's election in *Il Sussidiario*, an online journal close to Communion and Liberation in Italy: http://www.ilsussidiario.net/News/Cronaca/2013/3/14/PAPA-Bergoglio-ecco-cosa-c-entra-Don-Giussani-con-me/373016/.

3. See Alberto Melloni, *L'inizio di papa Ratzinger* (Turin: Einaudi, 2005), 17; Massimo Faggioli, *Breve storia dei movimenti cattolici* (Rome: Carocci, 2008), 98.

4. See Jamie Manson, "One of Pope Francis' Allegiances Might Tell Us Something about the Church's Future," *National Catholic Reporter*, March 15, 2013, http://ncronline.org/blogs/grace-margins/one-pope-francis-allegiances-might-tell-us-something-about-churchs-future.

5. See John W. O'Malley, *The Jesuits: A History from Ignatius to the Present* (Lanham, MD: Rowman & Littlefield, 2014); Raymond A. Schroth, *The American Jesuits: A History* (New York: NYU Press, 2007).

6. About this, see Paul Vallely, *Pope Francis: Untying the Knots* (London: Bloomsbury, 2013), 37–61; Austen Ivereigh, *The Great Reformer: Francis and the Making of a Radical Pope* (New York: Holt, 2014), 165–209.

7. Pope Francis, Address at the Vigil of Pentecost with the Ecclesial Movements, May 18, 2013, http://www.laici.va/content/laici/en/le-parole-di-papa-francesco/vegliadipentecoste2013.html.

8. Pope Francis, Homily at Pentecost Mass with the Ecclesial Movements, May 19, 2013, http://www.laici.va/content/laici/en/le-parole-di-papa-francesco/Pentecoste2013.html.

9. About this, see Massimo Faggioli, *Sorting Out Catholicism: A Brief History of the New Ecclesial Movements* (Collegeville, MN: Liturgical Press, 2014), 129–37.

10. See *Insegnamenti di Benedetto XVI* 2, no. 1 (2006): 757–65.

11. Pope Francis, apostolic exhortation *Evangelii Gaudium*, November 24, 2013, par. 28–29.

12. Pope Francis, Message to Participants in the 13th Meeting of the Basic Ecclesial Communities in Brazil (Juazeiro do Norte, Diocese of Crato, 7–11 January 2014), https://w2.vatican.va/content/francesco/en/letters/2013/documents/papa-francesco_20131217_comunita-ecclesiali-base.html.

13. Pope Francis, Address to Representatives of the Neocatechumenal Way, February 1, 2014, http://w2.vatican.va/content/francesco/en/speeches/2014/february/documents/papa-francesco_20140201_cammino-neocatecumenale.html.

14. See Massimo Faggioli, "The Neocatechumenate and Communion in the Church," *Japan Mission Journal* 65, no. 1 (Spring 2011): 46–53.

15. Pope Francis, Address to Members of the Neocatechumenal Way, March 6, 2015, http://w2.vatican.va/content/francesco/en/speeches/2015/march/documents/papa-francesco_20150306_cammino-neocatecumenale.html.

16. Francis had received in audience the parish priests of the diocese of Rome just two days before, March 6, 2014.

17. See *Un prêtre contre la mafia. Don Luigi Ciotti. Entretiens avec Nello Scavo et Daniele Zappalà* (Paris: Bayard, 2015).

18. Papa Francesco, Incontro con i partecipanti alla veglia di preghiera promossa dalla fondazione "Libera" nella parrocchia di San Gregorio VII in Roma (21 marzo 2014), https://press.vatican.va/content/salastampa/en/bollettino/pubblico/2014/03/21/0196/00434.html.

19. Pope Francis, Address to the Participants in the World Meet-

ing of Popular Movements, October 28, 2014, http://w2.vatican.va/
content/francesco/en/speeches/2014/october/documents/papa-fran
cesco_20141028_incontro-mondiale-movimenti-popolari.html.

20. Pope Francis, Address to Participants in the 37th National Con-
vocation of the Renewal in the Holy Spirit, Rome Olympic Stadium,
June 1, 2014, http://w2.vatican.va/content/francesco/en/speeches/2014/
june/documents/papa-francesco_20140601_rinnovamento-spirito-
santo.html.

21. Ibid.

22. Ibid.

23. Pope Francis, Address to Members of the "Catholic Fraternity
of Charismatic Covenant Communities and Fellowships," October 31,
2014, http://w2.vatican.va/content/francesco/en/speeches/2014/october
/documents/papa-francesco_20141031_catholic-fraternity.html.

24. Ibid. For the reference to the "ecumenism of blood," see also
the address to the members of the Renewal of the Holy Spirit on July
3, 2015: Papa Francesco, discorso al movimento del Rinnovamento
nello Spirito, http://w2.vatican.va/content/francesco/it/speeches/2015/
july/documents/papa-francesco_20150703_movimento-rinnovamento-
spirito.html (available only in Italian, Spanish, and Portuguese).

25. Address of Pope Francis to the Sant'Egidio Community, June 15,
2014, https://w2.vatican.va/content/francesco/en/speeches/2014/june/
documents/papa-francesco_20140615_comunita-sant-egidio.html.

26. Pope Francis, Address to Participants in the Third World Congress of Ecclesial Movements and New Communities, November 22,
2014, http://w2.vatican.va/content/francesco/en/speeches/2014/novem-
ber/documents/papa-francesco_20141122_convegno-movimenti-ecclesi
ali.html.

27. Pope Francis, Address to Members of the Communion and Liberation movement, March 7, 2015, http://w2.vatican.va/content/francesco/
en/speeches/2015/march/documents/papa-francesco_20150307_comu
nione-liberazione.html.

28. Ibid.

29. Ibid.

30. See Robi Ronza, "CL dal papa: cronache da un incontro," *La
Nuova Bussola Quotidiana*, March 9, 2015, http://www.lanuovabq.it/it/
articoli-cl-dal-papacronachedi-un-incontro-12019.htm.

31. See Massimo Borghesi, "Cos'è successo veramente in Piazza
San Pietro," *Terre d'America*, March 14, 2015, http://www.terredamerica.
com/2015/03/14/il-papa-e-comunione-e-liberazione-cose-successo-vera
mente-piazza-san-pietro/. See also the fine intellectual biography of Fr. Luigi

Giussani by Massimo Borghesi, *Luigi Giussani. Conoscenza amorosa ed esperienza del vero. Un itinerario moderno* (Bari: Edizioni di Pagina, 2015).

32. See Pierangelo Sequeri, "Il Papa, i movimenti, la Chiesa: l'impossibile chiusura," *Avvenire*, March 9, 2015, http://www.avvenire. it/Commenti/Pagine/il-Papa-i-movimenti-la-chiesa-editoriale-sequeri. aspx.

33. About the idea of process in theology and in the Church, see Francis's long interview with Antonio Spadaro, SJ, for *Civiltà Cattolica*, published in English with the title "A Big Heart Open to God" in the printed edition of *America*, September 30, 2013, 15–38.

34. About this, see Massimo Faggioli, *Pope Francis: Tradition in Transition* (Mahwah, NJ: Paulist Press, 2015).

35. Walter Kasper, *Pope Francis' Revolution of Tenderness and Love*, trans. William Madges (Mahwah, NJ: Paulist Press, 2015), 38.

36. Ibid., 10.

BIBLIOGRAPHY

Abbruzzese, Salvatore. *Comunione e Liberazione. Identité catholique et disqualification du monde*. Paris: Cerf, 1989.

Alberigo, Giuseppe and Joseph A. Komonchak, eds. *History of Vatican II*. 5 vols. Maryknoll, NY: Orbis, 1995–2006.

Anuth, Bernhard Sven. *Der Neokatechumenale Weg: Geschichte, Erscheinungsbild, Rechtscharakter*. Würzburg: Echter, 2006.

Appleby, Scott R., and Emmanuel Sivan. *Strong Religion: The Rise of Fundamentalisms around the World*. Chicago: University of Chicago Press, 2003.

Ardigò, Achille, Costantino Cipolla, and Stefano Martelli. *Scouts oggi*. Rome: Borla, 1989.

La bellezza di essere cristiani. I movimenti nella Chiesa. Vatican City: Libreria Editrice Vaticana, 2007.

Berry, Jason, and Gerald Renner. *Vows of Silence: The Abuse of Power in the Papacy of John Paul II*. New York: Free Press, 2004.

Bianchi, Sandro, and Angelo Turchini, eds. *Gli estremisti di centro: Il neo-integralismo cattolico degli anni '70. Comunione e liberazione*. Rimini-Florence, 1975.

Blazquez, Ricardo. *Le comunità neocatecumenali. Discernimento teologico*. Edited by Ezechiele Pasotti. Cinisello B.: San Paolo, 1995.

Bonnín, Eduardo. *Historia de un carisma*. Madrid: Libroslibres, 2003.

Borghesi, Massimo. *Luigi Giussani. Conoscenza amorosa ed esperienza del vero. Un itinerario moderno*. Bari: Edizioni di Pagina, 2015.

Camisasca, Massimo. *Comunione e Liberazione. Le origini (1954–1968)*. Cinisello B.: San Paolo, 2001.

————. *Comunione e Liberazione. Il riconoscimento (1976–1984). Appendice 1985–2005*. Cinisello B.: San Paolo, 2006.

————. *Comunione e Liberazione. La ripresa (1969–1976)*. Cinisello B.: San Paolo, 2003.

Camisasca, Massimo, and Maurizio Vitali, eds. *I movimenti della Chiesa negli anni Ottanta*. Milan: Jaca Book, 1982.

Casanova, José. *Public Religions in the Modern World*. Chicago: University of Chicago Press, 1994.

Casella, Mario. *L'Azione Cattolica del Novecento. Aspetti, momenti, interpretazioni, personaggi*. Rome: AVE, 2003.

————. *L'Azione Cattolica nell'Italia contemporanea: 1919–1969*. Rome, AVE, 1992.

————. *Il magistero dei papi sull'Azione Cattolica. Da Pio IX a Francesco (1868–2013)*. Rome: AVE, 2014.

Castellano Cervera, Jesús. *Carismi per il terzo millennio. I movimenti ecclesiali e le nuove comunità*. Rome: OCD, 2001.

Cheroutre, Marie-Thérèse. *Le Scoutisme au féminin. Les Guides de France, 1923–1998*. Paris: Cerf, 2002.

Cholvy, Gérard. *Histoire des organisations et mouvements chrétiens de jeunesse en France (XIXe-XXe siècle)*. Paris: Cerf, 1999.

Cholvy, Gérard, and Marie-Thérèse Cheroutre, eds. *Le scoutisme. Quel type d'hommes et quel type de femmes? Quel type de chrétiens?* Paris: Cerf, 1994.

Congar, Yves. *Jalons pour une théologie du laïcat*. Paris: Cerf, 1954 (English trans. by Donald Attwater [Westminster, MD: Newman Press, 1957]).

Cuminetti, Mario. *Il dissenso Cattolico in Italia, 1965–1980*. Milan: Rizzoli, 1983.

Dadder, Anke M. *Comunione e Liberazione. Phänomenologie einer neuen geistlichen Bewegung*. Konstanz: UVK, 2002.

Davie, Grace. *Religion in Britain since 1945: Believing without Belonging*. Cambridge MA: Blackwell, 1994.

Dawson, Lorne L. *Comprehending Cults: The Sociology of New Religious Movements*. Toronto: Oxford University Press Canada, 1998 (2nd ed., 2006).

De Marco, Vittorio. *Storia dell'Azione Cattolica negli anni Settanta*. Rome: Città Nuova, 2007.

Eisenstadt, Shmuel N. *Fundamentalism, Sectarianism, and Revolution:*

The Jacobin Dimension of Modernity. Cambridge: Cambridge University Press, 1999.

Faggioli, Massimo. *Sorting Out Catholicism: Brief History of the New Ecclesial Movements* (English translation, expanded edition of *Breve storia dei movimenti cattolici*, Roma 2008). Collegeville MN, Liturgical Press, 2014.

Favale, Agostino. *Comunità nuove nella Chiesa*. Padova: Messaggero, 2003.

———, ed. *Movimenti ecclesiali contemporanei. Dimensioni storiche, teologico-spirituali ed apostoliche*. Rome: LAS, 1980 (4th ed., 1991).

Ferrari, Liliana. *L'Azione Cattolica in Italia dalle origini al pontificato di Paolo VI*. Brescia: Queriniana, 1982.

Fondi, Enzo M., and Michele Zanzucchi. *Un popolo nato dal Vangelo. Chiara Lubich e i Focolari*. Cinisello B.: San Paolo, 2003.

Formigoni, Guido. *L'Azione Cattolica Italiana*. Milan: Ancora, 1988.

Giammanco, Roberto, ed. *Ai quattro angoli del fondamentalismo. Movimenti politico-religiosi nella loro tradizione, epifania, protesta, regressione*. Scandicci, Florence: La Nuova Italia, 1993.

Giolo, Antonio, and Brunetto Salvarani. *I Cattolici sono tutti uguali? Una mappa dei movimenti della Chiesa*. Genova: Marietti, 1992.

Giordani, Igino. *La Chiesa della contestazione*. Rome: Città Nuova, 1970.

Giovagnoli, Agostino, ed. *1968 tra utopia e Vangelo. Contestazione e mondo cattolico*. Rome: AVE, 2000.

González Fernández, Fidel. *I movimenti. Dalla Chiesa degli apostoli a oggi*. Milan: Rizzoli, 2000.

Gruppo Italiano di Docenti di Diritto Canonico, ed. *Fedeli Associazioni Movimenti. XVIII Incontro di Studio (2–6 luglio 2001)*. Milan: Glossa, 2002.

Guérin, Christian. *L'utopie Scouts de France. Histoire d'une identité collective, Catholique et sociale 1920–1995*. Paris: Fayard, 1997.

Gutiérrez, Anastasio. *Cristiani senza sconto. Anatomia di un gruppo ecclesiale*. Rome: Pontificia Università Lateranense, 1980 (2nd ed., Rome: Gruppo Laico Seguimi, 2001).

Hanna, Tony. *New Ecclesial Movements*. New York: Alba House; Staten Island, NY: Society of St. Paul, 2006.

Hayes, Michael A., ed. *New Religious Movements in the Catholic Church*. New York: Continuum, 2005.

Hegge, Christoph. *Rezeption und Charisma. Der theologische und rechtliche Beitrag Kirchlicher Bewegungen zur Rezeption des Zweiten Vatikanische Konzils.* Würzburg: Echter, 1999.

——. *Il Vaticano II e i movimenti ecclesiali. Una recezione carismatica.* Rome: Città Nuova, 2001.

Hervieu-Léger, Danièle. *De la mission à la protestation. L'évolution des étudiants chrétiens en France (1965–1970).* Paris: Cerf, 1973.

——. *Le pèlerin et le converti. La religion en mouvement.* Paris: Flammarion, 1999.

——. *Vers un nouveau christianisme? Introduction à la sociologie du christianisme occidental.* Paris: Cerf, 1986.

Horn, Gerd-Rainer. *The Spirit of '68: Rebellion in Western Europe and North America, 1956–1976.* New York: Oxford University Press, 2007.

Kasper, Walter. *Pope Francis' Revolution of Tenderness and Love.* Translated by William Madges. Mahwah, NJ: Paulist Press, 2015.

Kepel, Gilles. *La Revanche de Dieu. Chrétiens, juifs et musulmans à la reconquête du monde.* Paris: Seuil, 1991 (*The Revenge of God: The Resurgence of Islam, Christianity, and Judaism in the Modern World.* Translated by Alan Braley [University Park: Pennsylvania State University Press, 1994]).

Landron, Olivier. *Les Communautés nouvelles. Nouveaux visages du catholicisme français.* Paris: Cerf, 2004.

Laneyrie, Philippe. *Les Scouts de France. L'évolution du Mouvement des origines aux annés 80.* Paris: Cerf, 1985.

Leahy, Brendan. *Ecclesial Movements and Communities: Origins, Significance, and Issues.* Hyde Park, NY: New City Press, 2011.

Lubich, Chiara, and Igino Giordani. *"Erano i tempi di guerra...". Agli albori dell'ideale dell'unità.* Rome: Città Nuova, 2007.

Maino, Paolo. *Il post-moderno nella Chiesa? Il Rinnovamento carismatico.* Cinisello B.: San Paolo, 2004.

Majocchi, Paola, and Vittoria Prisciandaro. *In cordata. La storia del gruppo Seguimi.* Padova: Messaggero, 2005.

Masters, Thomas, and Amy Uelmen. *Focolare: Living a Spirituality of Unity in the United States.* Hyde Park, NY: New City Press, 2011.

McDonnell, Kilian. *The Charismatic Renewal and Ecumenism.* New York: Paulist Press, 1978.

Morello, Giovanni, and Francesco Pieri, eds. *Documenti pontifici sullo Scautismo*. Milan: Ancora, 1991.

I movimenti nella chiesa. Atti del II colloquio internazionale. Vocazione e missione dei laici nella chiesa oggi. Milan: Nuovo Mondo, 1987.

Nabhan-Warren, Kristy. *The Cursillo Movement in America: Catholics, Protestants, and Fourth-Day Spirituality*. Chapel Hill: University of North Carolina Press, 2013.

O'Connor, Edward. *Le renouveau charismatique: Origines et perspectives*. Paris: Editions Beauchesne, 1975.

O'Malley, John W. *What Happened at Vatican II*. Cambridge, MA: Belknap Press of Harvard University Press, 2008.

Oschwald, Hanspeter. *Bibel, Mystik und Politik. Die Gemeinschaft Sant'Egidio*. Freiburg i.B.: Herder, 1998.

Panciera, Mario. *Il Rinnovamento nello spirito in Italia: Una realtà ecclesiale*. Rome: RnS, 1992.

Panvini, Guido. *Cattolici e violenza politica. L'altro album di famiglia del terrorismo italiano*. Venice: Marsilio, 2014.

Pelletier, Denis. *À la gauche du Christ. Les chrétiens de gauche en France de 1945 à nos jours*. Paris: Seuil, 2012.

Pontifical Council for the Laity, ed. *Movements in the Church*. Vatican City: Libreria Editrice Vaticana, 1999.

———. *I Movimenti ecclesiali nella sollecitudine pastorale dei Vescovi*. Vatican City: Libreria Editrice Vaticana, 2000.

Porteous, Julian. *New Wine and Fresh Skins: Ecclesial Movements in the Church*. Leominster, Herefordshire: Gracewing, 2010.

Preglau-Hämmerle, Susanne, ed. *Katholische Reformbewegungen Weltweit*. Innsbruck-Wien: Tyrolia, 2012.

Un prêtre contre la mafia. Don Luigi Ciotti. Entretiens avec Nello Scavo et Daniele Zappalà. Paris: Bayard, 2015.

Preziosi, Ernesto. *Obbedienti in piedi. La vicenda dell'Azione Cattolica in Italia*. Turin: SEI, 1996.

Ranaghan, Kevin, and Dorothy Ranaghan. *Catholic Pentecostals*. Paramus, NJ: Paulist Press, 1969.

Ratzinger, Joseph (Pope Benedict XVI). *New Outpourings of the Spirit: Movements in the Church*. San Francisco: Ignatius, 2007.

Riccardi, Andrea. *Sant'Egidio, Rome et le monde. Entretiens avec Jean-Dominic Durand et Régis Ladous*. Paris: Beauchesne, 1996 (Translated by Peter Heinegg as *Sant' Egidio, Rome, and the World*. London: St. Pauls, 1999).

Robertson, Edwin. *The Fire of Love: A Life of Igino Giordani, "Foco," 1894–1980*. London: New City, 1989.

Rovello, Alessandro. *La morale e i movimenti ecclesiali*. Bologna: EDB, 2013.

Rusconi, Gian Enrico, and Chiara Saraceno. *Ideologia religiosa e conflitto sociale*. Bari: De Donato, 1970.

Saresella, Daniela. *Cattolici a sinistra. Dal modernismo ai giorni nostri*. Rome-Bari: Laterza, 2011.

———. *Dal Concilio alla contestazione. Riviste cattoliche negli anni del cambiamento, 1958–1968*. Brescia: Morcelliana, 2005.

Sauer, Joseph, ed. *Lebenswege des Glaubens: Berichte über Mönchtum heute, Gemeinschaften Charles de Foucaulds, Fokolar-Bewegung, Gemeinschaften christlichen Lebens, Schönstatt-Bewegung, Équipes Notre-Dame*. Freiburg i.B.: Herder, 1978.

Schirripa, Vincenzo. *Giovani sulla frontiera. Guide e Scout cattolici nell'Italia repubblicana (1943–1974)*. Rome: Studium, 2006.

Secondin, Bruno. *I nuovi protagonisti, movimenti, associazioni, gruppi nella Chiesa*. Cinisello B.: San Paolo, 1991.

Sica, Mario. *Storia dello scautismo in Italia*. Florence: La Nuova Italia, 1973 (4th ed., Rome: Fiordaliso, 2006).

Steinmaus-Pollak, Angelika. *Das als katholische Aktion organisierte Laienapostolat: Geschichte seiner Theorie und seiner kirchen-rechtlichen Praxis in Deutschland*. Würzburg: Echter, 1988.

Sullivan, Francis A. *Charisms and Charismatic Renewal: A Biblical and Theological Study*. Eugene, OR: Wipf and Stock, 2004.

Torcivia, Mario. *Guida alle nuove comunità monastiche italiane*. Casale M.: Piemme, 2001.

———. *Il segno di Bose*. Casale M.: Piemme, 2003.

Traniello, Francesco, and Giorgio Campanini, eds. *Dizionario storico del movimento cattolico in Italia, 1860–1980*. 3 vols. Casale Monferrato and Genova: Marietti, 1980–1995.

Tranvouez, Yvon. *Catholiques d'abord: Approches du mouvement catholique en France (XIXe–XXe siècle)*. Paris: Editions Ouvrières, 1988.

Zadra, Barbara. *I movimenti ecclesiali e i loro statuti*. Rome: Pontificia Università Gregoriana, 1997.

Zimmerling, Peter. *Die charismatischen Bewegungen. Theologie—Spiritualität—Anstöße zum Gespräch*. Göttingen: Vandenhoeck & Ruprecht, 2001.

INDEX